The Ramblings of a Rustic Copper

Brian Walter Wood

First Published in 2013
by Write Now! Publications
14 Hambrook Close,
Great Whelnetham,
Bury St Edmunds,
Suffolk IP30 0UX

All the stories in this publication are true with the exception of a couple which I have put in Italics. However some of the other stories have been slightly modified to give a more coherent picture of the circumstances.

Where I have referred to other police officers or members of the public, in most instances I have used a fictitious name to prevent embarrassment or distress

First Edition

ISBN: 0957020236
ISBN-13: 978-0957020238

This book is dedicated to my wife Gerry and my daughters Carolyn & Beverley, who after years of listening to my 'ramblings', have finally persuaded me to put my memories down on paper.

ACKNOWLEDGMENTS

I would like to thank Jez Reichmann for his help with the art work and patience in helping Carolyn to produce this book into the format you see today.

INTRODUCTION

Born in 1933 on a fairly isolated farm in rural Buckinghamshire I had a very sheltered early life. Due to illness I missed my final three years at school, therefore exams did not figure in my early years so there was quite a gap in my education. Was I destined for a mundane life? Well, as the following stories will tell, my life has been far from boring, in fact it has been quite exciting.

Up to the age of eighteen my life could be considered to be dull, but two years National Service as a soldier serving in the Canal Zone during the Suez Crisis proved to be an eye opener. From a farmer's boy, a country bumpkin, to a soldier serving abroad within eight weeks broadened my horizons somewhat rapidly. A culture shock to the system.

HOW IT ALL BEGAN

Perhaps a better title for this book would be "How on earth did I manage to become a police officer" ?

Indeed, when considering my earlier background, how on earth did I become a copper? The son of a small farmer (it was the farm that was small, not my Dad), in a fairly isolated place called Stockgrove in Buckinghamshire.

I have two older brothers and a younger sister and we lived in a very sheltered environment until I was eighteen years of age when I received my call-up papers to join the army. I was shy in the extreme.

So what had I going for me if I was to be a police officer, certainly not education?

When I was aged thirteen, I had acute appendicitis that had turned gangrenous, I was near death's door when I was taken to the Luton and Dunstable Hospital and it's here I spent the next thirteen weeks.

This was followed by well over a year's convalescence on the south coast of England. I did not go back to school and I certainly did not pass any examinations. I had no educational qualifications whatsoever so my future career seemed destined to be of a humdrum nature.

Shy, unfit and uneducated are not the qualities required of a police officer. It could be said that I was the original village idiot.

My two brothers had motorcycles, and with our lodgers, Mike Hennesey and John Chapman and a couple of tearaways from the local villages, they terrorised the local populace. They were not far short of being Hells Angels, much to the annoyance of the local police who often called at the farm to issue cautions. I had to join those scallywags as soon as possible.

Aged sixteen, I purchased an old clapped out 125cc BSA Bantam, I was now a Hells Angel, well, as near as possible as I could get - a skinny 16 year old on an small ancient motorbike!

By some miracle none of us 'Hells Angels' were involved in a serious accident or prosecuted by the police whom we regarded as the enemy.

As I mentioned earlier I was extremely shy as this little tale will tell. My two brothers got themselves girlfriends, so I had to have one.

I met this girl, Margaret and started to court her, well, kind of. About twice a week I was allowed to visit her parents' house. Her father worked at the sewage works on the A5 near Hockliffe and lived in a cottage next to the sewage works so our romance had a sort of aroma about it.

We used to sit in this little cottage, side by side on the settee, about a foot apart, with her Dad in his chair smoking his pipe, reading the paper and listening to the radio, her Mum would sit in her chair knitting.

It was always quiet in that room. With my only worldly knowledge being about turnips, BSA Bantams and chickens, after I had said a few words to my new girlfriend my scintillating conversation soon dried up.

About 9:00 p.m. her dad would allow my girlfriend and I to have ten minutes together outside to say goodnight and as soon as that ten minutes was up he would be at the door hollering at her to come in.

We would stand under a tree against which I had

propped my motor bike and just talk.

After two or three months I made the first move to progress our courtship by putting my arm round her waist. Phew, what excitement, I was quivering all over!

About a month or so later my girlfriend took the initiative, got hold of my hand and put it on her bosom. I was touching an intimate part of a woman! I went into a state of deep shock. I snatched my hand away as if it had been put in a furnace, jumped on my bike and was gone, I am sure that little Bantam reached 60 mph along the A5. That was the end of my first romance.

As a footnote, about fifty or so years later I was at my eldest brother's fiftieth wedding anniversary at Leighton Buzzard. My brother by then, was a successful businessman, president of the Rotary Club and a senior member of the Freemasons. (His 'Hells Angels' days were well into the past.)

After dinner he took me around the tables and introduced me to his distinguished guests. He introduced me to a lady and said, "You will remember Margaret", I must have looked mystified. He said "Margaret Sawyer, you used to court her". Memories came flooding back, particularly our last night together.

She looked at me and gave an enigmatic smile. She knew what I was thinking and I knew what she was thinking. As she put her hand out to shake hands I had a vivid memory of where my hand was the last time they touched, was she going to put it on her bosom again? I was momentarily in a state of panic. If my old BSA Bantam had been outside I might have done another runner.

I must admit, after all those years the memory caused my ears to go red, yes I am still a bit shy.

My sister Mary, aged about 11 or 12 years was leading a cow through the village of Great Brickhill when the vicar, passing the time of day, said,

"Good morning young girl, where are you taking the cow?" Mary said,

"To see the bull".

The vicar, somewhat shocked said, "Good heavens, that's not the job for a girl, cannot your father or one of your brothers do it?"

To which Mary replied,

"Oh no, it has to be the bull".

Two years national service mostly spent on active service in the Canal Zone did not improve my education very much but I did learn the hard facts of life, and some attributes such as smartness, loyalty, integrity and discipline. These must have rubbed off on me. I also managed to pass my Army Third Class Certificate of Education, my only formal qualification.

In 1953 and shortly after I had completed my National Service I started courting a girl called Gerry who was later to become my wife, but before that could happen I had to undergo quite a strict interview with my prospective father-in-law.

Les Heaword was a warrant officer in the Royal Air Force, and I believe he was somewhat dismayed that his only daughter Geraldine was showing too much interest in me.

One day I mumbled to him the word engagement. He was not impressed. I had been a lowly private in the Army, 'one of the brown jobs' was the term he used to describe me, and then a van driver whilst he was shortly to be commissioned in the Royal Air Force.

With my brothers and friends we were still a gang of motorcyclists and up to the usual high jinks. After my time in the army I purchased a proper motorbike, a BSA 500cc Gold Star, I was one step nearer to being a real Hells Angel.

This did not enamour me to my prospective father in law. He told me in no uncertain terms that if I was to entertain any thoughts of marriage to his daughter I had to change my lifestyle and have a job with a future.

My girlfriend's Dad suggested going back in the army, I said no. He suggested I joined the Royal Air Force, I said no. He suggested the Fire Brigade, I said no. I did not like heights. He then suggested the police force, the enemy, I said no. Then he mentioned this was a good job with security, good pay, allowances, pension, and a police house thrown in. That made me think, it was not such a bad suggestion after all, that I decided to take it up.

My motorcycling mates were horrified when I told them of my intentions. I was going to join the enemy! But the desire to share my life with Gerry overrode my wilder instincts.

I obtained the necessary application form, and then saw I had to have someone of high standing in the community to vouch for my good character!

What good character? Who did I know? Then I had a brilliant idea, I went to Linslade police station and asked to see Inspector Albert King.

Confronting this man of high standards, the conversation went something like this,

"What do you want boy?"

I said,

"I want you to endorse my application as to my good character so I can join the police".

He said,

"Why should I do that, I don't know who you are",

I replied,

"But I know who you are, you used to dance with my mother".

He asked somewhat guardedly,

"Who is your mother",

I said,

"Millie Wood".

After pondering over this for a minute or so he

finally said,

"Give me the form, for your damn cheek I will endorse it".

At this point it would be appropriate to comment on Inspector Albert King. A couple of years later, as a constable I was in court when I saw him in action. In those early days and before the Crown Prosecution Service came into being, the inspector would act as prosecuting officer, present the evidence, cross-examine witness, etc.

Inspector Albert King gave the opening address, presented the evidence and after this was over, in his closing speech, he told the magistrates in very firm terms that the offender was guilty as charged and what the appropriate penalty should be.

The magistrates without hesitation agreed and imposed the penalty as suggested, or perhaps I should say was ordered to by the inspector. Unbelievable today.

Rogers and Hammerstein in their opera, 'The Pirates of Penzance' wrote a line, "A policeman's lot is not a happy one". This may be true but I do know that after thirty years' service a policeman will have experienced a huge number of emotions, from happiness, satisfaction, to dread, fear, and then to outright terror.

There can be few careers in this world of ours that can generate so many emotions. Some of these emotions can be anticipated or expected and some are thrust upon us without warning.

During my service I have experienced most, if not all of the above mentioned emotions, with many more besides. Training helps to prepare officers to overcome some of these.

I was fortunate to have served with the army for two years before joining the police so was hardened somewhat to the hard knocks that life can throw at us.

THE POLICE

Policing, when I joined in 1955, bears little resemblance to that which is the norm in the police force of today, particularly as regards to discipline and respect by the public.

It was a very strict regime, for example, if a

constable on a day off wanted to visit his relatives in a neighbouring town, he had to make written application to his Superintendent for permission to leave the beat where he worked. He may have worked an eight hour day but he was in effect on duty twenty four hours a day.

When I applied for permission to get married a report was sent from Buckinghamshire Constabulary to Bedfordshire Constabulary requesting a senior officer to visit my prospective wife and her parents at Leighton Buzzard to see if they were suitable to be related to their very young and new constable.

My prospective in-laws house was examined and the people there questioned at depth to see that they did or did not have criminal connections, and were not involved in the liquor licensing or betting trade.

Incidentally, bearing the above in mind I have no doubt that when I first applied to join the police they had most probably done a background check on me and my family and may well have known about my aspiration to be a Hells Angel, and of the cautions issued to me, but I was not aware of any of these checks.

Another circumstance I remember was that after

I got married in August 1955 and before I was allocated a police house, I was stationed at High Wycombe in Buckinghamshire and my wife lived at Leighton Buzzard in Bedfordshire so it was necessary for me to submit a report asking for permission every time I was off duty to travel out of the county to see her.

When due for the annual two week holiday and it was the wish of the officer to, say go to the seaside, or tour, he had to submit a report listing all the holiday addresses and telephone numbers of places he may be staying at.

Under no circumstances was a police officer allowed to take a part-time job or to be associated in any way with the betting or the licensed premises trade.

I recall one of the constables at Aylesbury, Frank Wright, who bought a car (his parents had a newsagent's and no doubt helped with its purchase.) He was chastised as the only officer at Aylesbury in the mid 1950's that owned a car was Superintendent Bill Tomlin.

One of the sergeants really berated him for the impudence of owning a car when none of the higher ranking Sergeants had such a luxury.

Frank had not broken any police regulations so the senior officers could not do anything about it.

THE FIRST STEPS TO BEING A POLICE CONSTABLE

On the 14th March 1955 I presented myself at the Buckinghamshire Constabulary recruiting department at Walton Grove, Aylesbury where I and the seven other potential police officers were given a medical and some tests.

I passed the medical and managed to satisfy the recruiting officer on all the tests except spelling. Out of 120 fairly long words I got just about a quarter right. What a dismal showing! Was my future career over already?

The recruiting inspector Jim Hipgrave, after some deliberation told me that they would take a chance with me providing, on my side, I made a determined effort to improve my spelling. I was sent with the other seven brand new Bucks officers in our new uniforms with shiny buttons to the Police Training College at Eynsham Hall, near Witney, Oxfordshire for three months training.

In addition to all the classes and the comprehensive training given at the college, I also had to learn to spell. This was three months of intensive learning, a habit I had got out of since I was about 12 years old.

Help was provided by my prospective wife Gerry. During every weekend's leave we would walk round the fields of the farm I would spend practically every minute we could together with Gerry reading all the bigger words out of newspapers and books and I would spell them, later write them out several times, whatever, as long as I got them right. I also had to take in the criminal definitions and powers of arrest. An educational mountain.

At Eynsham Hall, we had an exam at the end of each month and of the 35 officers from the various forces I finished bottom but two after the first month. At the end of the second month I was fifteenth and at the end of the third and final month I was third in my class. Not a bad achievement for a country yokel. I had, at last, learnt to learn.

At Eynsham Hall, I made many friends but my

closest was Jimmy Woodrow who came from Bungay, Suffolk. We remained good friends during our respective 30 years of service and still keep in touch. He had a wry sense of humour.

I recall on an observation test we were asked to give the name of the commandant's house that was near the entrance to the college. Jimmy did not know so he put down "The Nightingale's Harem." The commandant was not amused. His name was Nightingale.

Some years later and when Jimmy Woodrow worked at the police headquarters at Ipswich, his Chief Constable complained to him that he was so busy there were not enough hours in the day, so after the Chief Constable had left his office for the day, Jimmy sneaked in took his wall clock home, painted out the hours and very carefully painted in thirteen hours.

It was a week before the Chief Constable realised what had happened and Jimmy was called in for a mild reprimand.

One of the easiest part of the Eynsham Hall routine was the morning parades, a piece of cake for me having served two years in the army. Some of those who did not have military training found marching hard going.

I learnt First Aid, how to give evidence in court, how to take a statement from a witness, make a statement, make out reports, and I had to learn lots of definitions of the various acts of parliament and powers of arrest that I would later be expected to execute. We also had dummy courts and this was an ordeal for this country lad who had never spoken in public or under these circumstances before.

Back at the Buckinghamshire Constabulary headquarters, and true to his word, after the expense of sending me on the three month course, kitting me out in uniform and all the other costs of recruitment, the recruiting inspector gave me a 120 word spelling test. I got about 100 right. What an improvement, and true to the promise I made to myself, I was to become a police officer with the Buckinghamshire Constabulary.

I still remember taking the oath of office on a bible in the presence of a Justice of the Peace.

"I, Brian Wood do solemnly swear that I will serve our Sovereign Lady the Queen in the office of constable in the County of Buckingham without fear, favor, affection, malice or ill will, and I will

carry out my duties faithfully according to law."

I was then given my posting, it was High Wycombe. This was definitely not to my liking but I was given no alternative.

At this point I should mention that after five years, of the eight constables from the Buckinghamshire Constabulary recruited the same time as I was, me, the doubtful one due to my poor spelling and limited education was the only one still serving.

Alan Soar left to join the Rhodesian Police, Reggie, I will not mention his surname as he is still about, had an affair with a Sergeant's wife, and was dismissed. Another officer was given the choice of giving up his girlfriend; a high class prostitute, or resign, he resigned. One, who was posted to Marlow, took to walking the streets accompanied by an unmarried woman with her two children.

The constable at Marlow was a funny chap; he used to wear his Salvation Army uniform when he left Eynsham Hall at weekends to meet the unmarried lady. His relationship was frowned upon. He was pressurised to leave the force. I do not recall what happened to the other three.

HIGH WYCOMBE

Life in the police force in the 1950's was vastly different to what it is today. As mentioned earlier discipline was very strict and I was soon to feel the full force of it from my senior officers.

I was posted to High Wycombe in May 1955 and my first two weeks there was spent on the beat with a very senior constable who was supposed to show me the ropes, but he seemed to spend more time scrounging from shops, something I vowed I would never do.

I recall the superintendent's favourite trick was to stop an officer and say, "I am a member of the public, I have just stopped you, direct me to Hughenden Road." If you could not give clear and concise instructions you got a bollocking. Needless to say my local map was perused a lot, both on and off duty. In addition I had to study all the training manuals, and of course I had to learn to type.

We had to do our own reports and I bought a really ancient typewriter and learnt two finger typing. I am still a two finger typist but can rattle off the words quite quickly on my computer.

The Superintendent used to hold monthly parades, which all available police officers had to attend. He would pick out an officer and show him a photograph of a local criminal and if an officer was unable to identify him then there was a lot of shouting and bawling. Then he would ask a hapless constable to give a power of arrest for a specific offence. More shouting and bawling.

All officers dreaded these parades, even more dreaded was being picked out and made to look a fool, or at least an incompetent, but the experience kept you on your toes.

I distinctly remember my first day on the beat on my own. I was working two - ten evening shift and my beat was the town centre, just my luck. As I left the police station I was full of apprehension. What if something serious occurred that I had not been trained to deal with? Would I be able to cope, what if there was a serious accident how would the sight of badly injured bodies affect me?

There were so many of these thoughts going through my mind that I lingered for a while behind the town hall, then a sense of duty motivated me to enter the High Street and start my patrol.

From then on my confidence built up and I coped with all the minor problems that came my way that day.

Generally, my time at High Wycombe passed peacefully and few major problems were experienced. I do recall chasing a thief who had run across the top of some buildings in the High Street. Someone else caught and arrested him.

I was so chuffed with my first offence, a lad riding a cycle without lights, that the next morning I cycled to Marlow, about five miles each way, to share my exciting adventure with the colleague who was with me at Eynsham, the one I mentioned earlier who was in the Salvation Army. I was dismayed when he told me he had made two reports!

On another occasion I got called to a very bad accident when a fully laden lorry coming down Marlow Hill had brake failure, the lorry hit a building at the bottom of the hill and the driver was killed.

Fortunately I was with an experienced officer who in effect dealt with the accident and the inquest whilst I learnt an awful lot about dealing with this type of situation.

In early August 1955 Gerry managed to get a message through asking me to be at a telephone box at a certain time. At the allotted time she called and said that I had three minutes to make up my mind, would I marry her the following Tuesday, six days hence.

The reason for this call was that I previously had discussed with Gerry's father the impending marriage to his daughter. Gerry's father was still in the R.A.F and in August 1955 was on leave from Cyprus. He had returned home and after his leave was to go back to Cyprus with his family, including Gerry. She did not want to go and her father said she could only remain in England if she was married, hence the telephone call to see if I agreed.

One of the most rapid decisions I have ever made was made that day. I said, "Yes." Then started the panic, in the five days I had to obtain the superintendent's permission to get married, change one rest day with a colleague so that I could be at the wedding the following Tuesday, buy a suit and then hastily arrange a honeymoon, one night in a hotel in Amersham, Buckinghamshire.

Gerry and her parents also had a lot of plans to make including getting a wedding dress, booking the church and obtaining a special marriage licence from the Bishop of St Albans. I do not know how she and her family managed it.

I must say that the police helped me as much as possible bearing in mind the short notice. They allowed me a two day honeymoon that was in effect two days annual leave I had to take from the annual two weeks allocation.

We were married at Leighton Buzzard Parish Church on the 9th August 1955, with the reception at Gerry's parent's house.

On return to duty after my honeymoon, Gerry spent a few days in my lodgings, 63 Green Street, High Wycombe. My landlord and landlady were a railwayman and a laundry lady respectively who were very understanding and made us both welcome.

I applied for a police house and this was granted the following October. Meanwhile, for most of the time I lived some 25 miles away from my wife.

AYLESBURY

We moved to Aylesbury in October 1955 and were allocated a house at 83 Stoke Road, a tiny terraced house with practically no creature comforts, no bathroom, no hot water, no electrical equipment, a few light bulbs, oh, and an outside toilet.

Originally owned by the London, Midland and Scottish Railways, it had been condemned by them as unfit for human habitation, so the Buckinghamshire Constabulary bought it for the housing of their constables.

But the house did have a large gas copper boiler that was used for washing our clothes and heating water for our weekly bath in a zinc tub.

The second bedroom was very damp with mould on the walls and a leaky roof. The police allowed us to take in police lodgers for which they paid us £2.50 per week for lodgings and two meals a day.

I recall that Tony Scowan (later an inspector at

Bracknell) was our first tenant, followed by Gwyn (Taffy) Blaken.

The house was in a poor state of repair, but help was at hand. In those days the Buckinghamshire Constabulary would help officers living in police houses with the cost of redecoration. The Police would pay for half the cost of the wallpaper and paint, the occupier was expected to pay the other half, and do the decorating themselves. The wallpaper I put up soon peeled off due to the damp walls, but I had tried my best.

What a difference to those living in council houses, houses that were often abused. I have known of instances when the occupants have removed all the internal doors and chopped them up for firewood. They had the houses decorated free by council workers every two to three years, paid for by the taxpayer of course.

DOZY DAVID

For a time John Brown was a constable on my shift; he was, if it was possible even dozier than I was, a real rustic. He was nick-named David Brown, after a tractor produced in those days that was very slow and ponderous, just like Constable Brown.

In the 1950's and 1960's it was procedure to stop all vehicles after 12 midnight and check out the occupants. This was not particularly time consuming as in those days few people travelled around at night.

The thinking behind this was that questions asked gave a pattern of people in vehicles travelling throughout the night in the Buckinghamshire county and elsewhere, a good crime prevention and detection measure.

Just after midnight, I met up with David Brown at the top of the High Street, after a few minutes, a car approached and David stopped it. The driver was asked where he had come from, he said,

"Bristol".

David asked him if he had seen anything unusual on the roads, and after a negative response, asked the driver where he was heading to, the driver said,

"Bury St Edmunds."

To which David replied, after digesting this bit of information for a short while,

"O'Ah, I didn't know he had died."

TURNING THE TABLES

On the first day I entered Aylesbury police station in October 1955 I met Sergeant John Matthews. He was an unsmiling and sombre so-and-so, a long streak of misery. He was a big chap with a high whining voice. He took an instant dislike to me, no, more of a hatred, and always gave me the dirty jobs and, criticised me at every opportunity.

Fortunately he was not my shift sergeant but

when shifts overlapped, or when he was relief sergeant he took every opportunity to make my life hell. I am sure he was trying to force me to resign.

He was stand-in sergeant on night shift towards the end of my two year probationary period. He went off duty at 2:00 a.m., so there was just Alan Jenkins the reserve constable and I, the beat constable on duty. Alan contacted me at my conference point at 3:00 a.m. and suggested I returned to the station.

On arrival at the station Alan showed me a copy of a report submitted by Sergeant Matthews to the superintendent about me. Sergeant Matthews suggested in the report that my service as a constable should be dispensed with as I was not of the right material, a waste of space, and was not fit to wear the uniform of a constable.

This news shattered me because Gerry and I were then in a police house and if we were kicked out we would be homeless, moneyless and jobless. Time to make a plan.

I gave a great deal of thought to this impending problem and sure enough a few days later I was called up in front of Superintendent Bill Tomlin and he told me of the contents of the report, I had a ready response. I reiterated my great desire and determination to be a good and efficient officer and related a number of good acts of police work I had performed. My arrests and offences reported was on par with that of other officers and no complaints had been made against me.

I also told the superintendent that I was held in good esteem by the other sergeants and constables. Now I really wanted to impress him, I told him that I was at an advanced stage on three correspondence courses, on police subjects, local and national politics and educational subjects, and shortly hoped to take my Sergeant's and Inspectors exams. I showed him the exam results, which I must say with some humility, were rather good.

Superintendent Bill Tomlin was a wily old bird and he obviously knew John Matthews better that I did, and no doubt he had conferred with the other sergeants. He made a quick decision and confirmed me in my appointment as a constable. What a relief, I was really in and could relax for the first time in two years.

Now let's move forward twelve years; I was by then a detective sergeant in charge of my own squad, the Motor Vehicle Investigation Branch.

Due to my expertise in these matters, one of my duties was to lecture at the Force Training Centre, Sulhamstead, Berkshire, on matters relating to stolen vehicles, topics including how to identify stolen vehicles, investigate insurance fraud, auto arson, document forgery, import and export of stolen vehicles and such like.

I gave these lectures on average once or twice a week to courses that variously consisted of probationers, CID officers of all ranks, inspectors, senior constables, newly promoted sergeants, senior sergeants, etc.

My lectures together with those given by a man from the Forensic Science Laboratories were always rated best in the usual course critiques mainly because of the good subject matter and some good visual aids.

As I entered the classroom of senior sergeants I looked at the twelve experienced and hardened sergeants, I saw Sergeant John Matthews sitting in the second row. He gave me a hard look, yes he recognised me as the probationer he tried to get rid of.

What pleasure I had in lecturing to my old

adversary, a sergeant who did not consider me fit enough to be a constable, I, now, higher up the ladder than he was, was to lecture him on how he could become a better and more efficient police officer. Revenge is sweet.

Incidentally, I passed both the Sergeant's and Inspector's exams at one sitting one year after the confirmation of my appointment as a constable.

INITIATION

Now returning to the timeline; Probationer police officers at Aylesbury were given a little unofficial initiation test during their first week of nights. Can you imagine what it is like to be the only constable on duty in a town the size of Aylesbury, all on your own with just your whistle and truncheon for comfort? The responsibility for the security and safety of the whole town's population of twenty five thousand residents rests on your young shoulders.

It is a very lonely job and in those days nothing moved after midnight and the only things that disturbed the peace was the wailing of cats, an occasional barking dog. It can be eerily quiet.

The strength of the police in Aylesbury in those days was nominal and it was normal for two or three officers to parade for duty on each shift, one was allocated office duty and the other two were beat officers. Needless to say those beats were big as it could include the surrounding villages, and a lot of leg work was involved.

About 4:00 a.m. one morning during my first week of nights, I was in Aylesbury High Street, I was tired, cold and truth be known walking in a kind of trance when right behind me there was god-awful crashing noise. My heart nearly stopped, I spun round not knowing what to expect. One of my colleagues had crept up, wrapped his handcuffs onto his truncheon and threw them up in the air so that they landed right behind me. It's hard to describe the initial feeling of terror that runs through your body after such an incident. It's a real wake up call.

I must admit later during my time at Aylesbury, I have played the same trick on other new probationers.

ACCIDENT ON TRING HILL

Whilst I was on patrol one evening Sergeant Mitchell picked me up in the police car and said we had to attend a bad accident at the top of Tring Hill, just our side of the Buckinghamshire/Hertfordshire border.

We arrived there and this is where I got a good bit of instruction in police work. One of the driver's had obviously been drinking and he failed to carry out the basic sobriety tests that were then used before the breathalyser was introduced. It was also obvious that he was the cause of the accident.

Sergeant Mitchell was a good instructor and he advised me how to carry out the sobriety tests as it was my first major accident and my first drunk driver. These were simple but effective tests and varied in different forces but were basically along the lines of:

Could the person walk in a straight line?

Could they place their finger tip to their nose?

Could they stand on one leg?

He then told me to arrest the driver and take him to Aylesbury police station where duty Inspector took over the charge procedure.

It's all right going through the motions of dealing with this type of incident in the classroom at Eynsham Hall, but a different kettle of fish when dealing with the real thing on the roadside with real members of the public.

I saw the case through the Magistrate's Court and then the Quarter Sessions to a successful conclusion.

THE SLOW WALK TO AYLESBURY

Police constables have to deal with lots of really unpleasant sights and I have to admit that during the first year of my service I saw only one dead body (an accident at High Wycombe), and up to the time of this incident I had not seen a really gruesome one, or attended a post mortem and subsequent inquest.

About 5:00a.m. one summer morning, Sergeant Jim Mellows received a call to go to Aylesbury railway station and there he learnt that the driver of the milk train that comes in about 4:30 a.m. each morning, had reported hitting a human body on the line somewhere between Stoke Mandeville and Aylesbury and bits of the body had adhered to the front of the train.

Jim telephoned the station and instructed me to take the station car to Stoke Mandeville railway station and walk the railway line towards the Aylesbury station and look out for the other parts of the body.

It would be two firsts for me, the first time I had driven a police car, and the first time I would see and have to deal with bits of a body. I looked forward to the first but dreaded the second.

I got the keys off the hook in the sergeant's office, went to the garage, the keys opened an Austin and operated the ignition so off I went. It was a nice car to drive.

At Stoke Mandeville railway station I locked the car and started a search of the four to five mile stretch of the railway, and I must admit I deliberately made a slow and thorough search and fortunately, the body was found just short of

Aylesbury railway station and by the time I got there it had been bagged up.

 I was very relieved as breakfast was not too far away and I am sure I would not have enjoyed it.

That was not the end of the incident. After retrieving the car from Stoke Mandeville I returned to Aylesbury, garaged the car and was then confronted by an irate traffic sergeant who came out of the headquarters control room that was next door to the police station.

Apparently I had taken a traffic patrol car instead of the station car and the two traffic officers who came on duty at 6:00 a.m. were bereft of a patrol car, a serious matter in the eyes of the traffic department. How was I to know? It was a coincidence that the keys fitted both cars.

NEVER DISOBEY AN ORDER

When I had been in the force for about six months, and to make life easier, I reached the stage when certain cunning ruses had been learnt from other officers. I had seen more senior constables taking advantage of situations, to their benefit, perhaps I should look at ways to make my life easier.

Whilst on nights I had been reserve officer at Aylesbury police station for the first three hours. This entailed answering the telephone switchboard, dealing with callers and sometimes a bit of filing and other paperwork.

Then, after the meal break (1:00 a.m. to 1:45 a.m.) we were sent out on the beat. I could never work out whether to call it a late supper or an early breakfast! Anyhow, I did something to incur the wrath of my relief sergeant Jim Mellows.

Now Jim was an ex-Coldstream Guardsman Sergeant Major. He was an imposing man both in stature and personality. He was a man who would not tolerate any foolish behaviour and he was a very strict disciplinarian, but utterly fair.

He gave me my conference points, the first at Stone Bridge at 3:00 a.m., some two and a half miles walk from the station, the next point at 4:00 a.m., was Bierton Post Office, another two and a half mile walk, and the third, a similar distance again, was the Picture House Kiosk at the top of Tring Road at 5:00 a.m. Then it would be a slightly shorter two miles back to the station to finish off the second half of my night duty.

I was dismayed that he was giving me such a hard time and was dreading almost a ten mile walk in the middle of the night. But a plan was starting to formulate in my head, I was beginning to learn a bit of cunning.

As I left the station Jim called out to me,

"Wood, don't take your bike."

How did he know, what was in my mind? In any event the thought of the very long walk overrode caution and as Jim was otherwise engaged I sneaked my bike out of the cycle shed, carried it up the steps behind the town hall and made my way to Stone Bridge on the Bicester Road.

In the unlikely event Jim would turn up for the 3:00 a.m. conference point, I dropped the bike down the bank and under the bridge.

In the days before mobile phones and radios, constables used to make conference points at certain telephone boxes at given times so that their senior officer could contact them if an incident had occurred or they were required for some other reason. We had to be at the conference point five minutes before the time given and remain for ten minutes.

On meeting at the conference point, the constable would report any incident that had happened and the sergeant would check his pocket book and sign it.

Jim drove up to Stone Bridge in the station van, an old Ford ten, dead on the dot of 2:55 a.m. I reported that it was 'all quiet' and then for the next ten minutes we stood there in utter silence. Then, to my amazement Jim said

"Get in."

Except for an emergency in those days' constables did not ride in police vehicles. He took me back to Aylesbury town centre, drove around a bit and then dropped me off in Bierton Road, Aylesbury with instructions to make my way to the next point at Bierton Post Office.

I just made it on time. After waiting the usual ten minutes I then found myself in a quandary, my bike was two and a half miles in one direction and my next point was two and a half miles in the opposite direction. The decision was easy; I had to make the conference point.

On arrival at the Picture House kiosk, I carried out the normal police 'duty' of pressing button B in the phone box. It's amazing how many people used the telephone in those days, did not get through, replaced the handset and forgot to press button B to get their money back. It would be unusual during a week of nights not to receive a small additional income from these phone boxes.

At 5:05 a.m. I set off for the police station, arriving at the station dead on six o'clock. I reported all was quiet and had nothing to report so Jim dismissed me.

As I was leaving the parade room, Jim called out, for the second time that morning,

"Wood, don't forget to pick up you bike at Stone Bridge".

I had well and truly been punished for disobeying an order as I had another two and a half mile walk in my own time, and after just finishing a punishing walk. I will never forget that little lesson.

Jim could have put me on a charge for disobeying an order but that was not Jim's way of doing things, unless the transgression was serious. It was 'Jim's Justice'. I suppose these days it would be called man management.

JUST A LITTLE MISTAKE

I can now recall what had upset Jim that night. Someone had handed in a found umbrella and I had duly entered it up in the found property book.

In his usual thorough way Jim had checked the found property book and he said to me,

"Wood, did you take in an item of found property earlier?"

I said,

"Yes sergeant, an umbrella".

He said,

"How did you know it belonged to a black woman?"

I replied, "I did not know it belonged to a black woman sergeant!"

He then asked,

"Why have you put 'a black woman's umbrella' in the found property book?"

I then realised my mistake. He slapped the book on the desk and told me to put it right. Another little lesson learnt.

WHAT'S IN A NUMBER?

In the 1950's, if a police officer was requested to give his full title to a member of the public, or indeed, when giving evidence in court, he would identify himself by giving his rank, number and name. For example, I would identify myself as Police Constable 160 Wood.

A new recruit joined the Buckinghamshire Constabulary just after me and his name was Tony Ball. Unbelievably, he was given the number one. So he would give his identity in court as Police Constable One Ball.

It was several months before the chiefs realised this could be a little bit embarrassing and he was given another number.

On the topic of police numbers, on joining the police in 1955 I was allocated the shoulder number 160. I left the police in May 1965 and re-joined in December 1966. On re-joining I tried to get my old number but it had been allocated to another officer so I was assigned the number of 306.

DEATH MESSAGE TO BRILL

The public do not realise what the police have to do during the course of their duty and the hardships they have to endure whilst they, the public, are asleep, warm and comfortable in their beds at night.

One winter's night, it had been snowing, about three inches lay on the ground, it had started to melt and then the slush froze leaving the roads covered in hard ruts of ice.

I was on the town centre beat when Sergeant Jim Mellows called me into the station. I thought perhaps he had a feeling of sympathy for me patrolling the beat in such bitterly cold weather.

No such luck.

Jim had received a call from another police force asking for a death message to be delivered to an address in Brill. Now Brill is a village at least fifteen miles from Aylesbury, at the top of a hill and the houses are mostly spread out with just a few streets.

Death messages, on almost every occasion cause shock and distress to the recipient(s) and have to be delivered with compassion and if possible the constable delivering the message will do what he can to alleviate their suffering. It is not a popular task and no police officer enjoys having to deliver such a message.

Jim told me I was to take the force motorbike, a BSA 500cc, and deliver the message. We did not have motorcycle kit in those days so all I had to wear was my greatcoat, woollen gloves (with cotton gloves inside) and a Corker helmet.

I set off from Aylesbury and the bike was slithering and sliding all over the A418 towards Thame, and then on the minor road through Grendon Underwood to Brill. It was a nightmare journey and seemed to take hours. Parts of my body were sweating from the exertion of keeping the bike upright and other parts, the extremities, were frozen to the extent I feared I might suffer from frostbite.

Eventually, I reached Brill about 4:30 a.m. but could not find the address. No street lights were on, the houses, many without numbers, were scattered over the hills that are a feature of Brill. At least I could walk about and get my circulation back.

Not a single house light was on. After a while I saw a window light up, I knocked at the door of the house and a man there fortunately knew the address I required and he came with me to the house.

The sad news was broken to the family and after making sure that there was someone to comfort the bereaved family, I had to make the very cold and arduous journey back to Aylesbury.

Jim did show some consideration for my frozen condition as on this occasion he sent me home early.

ALONE AND FRIGHTENED

Bereavement is a hard time for those left behind but one such incident I dealt with was particularly hard and harrowing.

I had to deal with the death of a man at a factory in the Bicester Road, Aylesbury. There were no suspicious circumstances. The man had died of a heart attack at the comparatively young age of about 50.

As the officer dealing with this sudden death the task of notifying the next of kin fell to me.

After obtaining the deceased's home address I first visited the deceased's neighbour where I established from her that the dead man had lived with his aged father who was wheelchair bound, and the son had been the sole carer for his father for about twenty years. There were no other relatives.

With the neighbour, I called at the address and on hearing the sad news the father was extremely distraught, it was heartrending to hear him cry so much. He had no-one to look after him. He had no one in the world to whom he could turn.

Arrangements were made with social services to look after him and eventually he ended up in a nursing home.

I used to visit him occasionally at the home and other than one of his former neighbours we were the only visitors. He did not live for long. He had nothing to live for.

NEGLECT OF DUTY

I was on duty in the Market Square, Aylesbury, when about midnight one cold and frosty night a passing lorry driver told me that he had seen a car in the ditch between Winslow and Aylesbury. He had made a quick search but did not see anyone at the scene. I telephoned the information through to the duty sergeant, John Walsh.

I went in for my meal break about 1:00 a.m. and afterwards asked the sergeant if the incident had been dealt with and he said he would deal with it shortly.

After my meal I was posted outside the town, then about 4:30 a.m. John Walsh turned up in the police van at the Picture House Kiosk in the Tring Road, told me to get in and we drove to the scene of the accident, arriving some four and a half hours after I reported it to him.

We arrived at the scene to see an Austin A90 in the ditch. I noted that the sunshine roof was missing, rather strange as it was well below freezing. There did not appear to be anyone at the scene despite the fact that the car had hit the ditch with a huge impact.

I walked along the road for about 100 yards looking for anything in the ditch or a way through the hedge. I was also looking for the sunshine roof. I saw a gap in the hedge and entered the field and walked back in the opposite direction to where the car was. There I found the body of a man with a broken neck. His name was MacDonald Daly, a well-known dog breeder and television celebrity at the time.

Alongside was a woman; she was alive but unconscious. I shouted to John Walsh what I had found and he went off to Winslow to telephone for an ambulance (still no radio in the police van at this time).

It would appear that on impact the occupants had both been catapulted through the roof knocking the sunshine roof off. It must have been a horrific accident as the two occupants were some ten feet into the field and they had gone over a six foot high thick hedge.

They had been lying there so long that frost was gathering on the couple, the woman was later identified as the man's wife.

I stayed with her until the ambulance from Aylesbury arrived some thirty minutes later. Despite my first aid training there was nothing I could do for her other than put her in the recovery position and cover her with my greatcoat to keep her as warm as possible.

That poor woman had been there almost five hours and almost died, and I blame the sergeant for not turning out earlier. Although the records showed the police delay and there was an inquest, no action was taken against the sergeant.

The woman did regain consciousness and I later visited her in hospital to tie up some loose ends in relation to the accident and she fortunately made a full recovery.

John Walsh reached a high rank in the police force so this incident did not hold back his promotion.

If I had made a complaint against him it could well of jeopardised his career, but then, as a sergeant he could have made my life awkward so that, as a young constable he indirectly influenced me, rightly or wrongly to keep my mouth shut.

CAUGHT DEAD TO RIGHTS

In my early days in the police force, constables were not allowed to have other jobs or do anything else other than be a constable.

One of our constables at Aylesbury was Percy Parker, a bit of a 'fly boy' and someone I did not get on with.

One morning I was in the Tring Road near the Hazel, Watson and Viney paper works standing alongside Sergeant Jim Mellows when Jim said in his clipped military manner,

"Stand to attention constable",

Then he barked,

"Prepare to salute",

I then saw a funeral cortège approaching from the town centre direction.

As it slowly passed Jim shouted,

"Salute".

We both saluted smartly, as only a guardsman and infantry man could. (Policemen today do not show the same respect for the dead in the same way).

As the hearse passed there was Percy in the driver's seat, resplendent in a smart green uniform and peaked cap. I saw Jim's eyes following him as the hearse passed, and Percy, seeing the sergeant had a look of terror on his face, or perhaps it was his funeral face. Whatever, he knew he was in trouble.

I never did find out what punishment Percy received but I do know he was not officially disciplined. No doubt 'Jim's Justice' was duly dispensed.

Percy did not last long in the job as he was found to be having an affair with a married woman who worked in the local laundry. Adultery was an instant dismissible offence in those early days.

A SMART OFFICER

Police constable Frank Read was at Aylesbury when I was posted there in 1955. He was dapper and smart in appearance and was a very good copper, both on the beat and with the usual paperwork. He was about ten years older than me so would have served in the armed forces during World War Two.

I do not know for what reason, but in the late 1950's for six months he was recalled to the Army. It must have been for a very important reason as police work came before the army reserve service.

One day sergeant Jim Mellows and I were walking, or perhaps I should say patrolling along

Aylesbury High Street when, who was approaching us from the opposite direction but Frank in his military uniform, complete with Sam Browne belt, carrying a swagger stick and gloves, with a captain's insignia on his shoulders.

As he neared us Jim, who recognised him, gave Frank a smart salute. Fancy a police sergeant saluting one of his constables! But that was typical of Jim, always correct.

Frank Read on re-joining the police was soon promoted to sergeant and moved to Slough and I did not see him for many years.

Our paths met one day when I, then a Detective Sergeant went to Slough police station to see someone about a young tearaway.

The Police Juvenile Liaison Officer was Sergeant Frank Read. We had a good time reminiscing about old times at Aylesbury.

I was however surprised that an officer with Frank's undoubted abilities did not go any further than sergeant. Perhaps he, like me, did not wish to take on promotion.

A SHARP ENCOUNTER OR TWO

Knife crime in the 1950's and 1960's was not as frequent as it is today (2013), in fact it was quite a rarity. There were villains around carrying knives but the usual outcome was a bit of slashing, not stabbing to death as seems to be normal these days.

One late evening I was patrolling the Market Square, Aylesbury, when I got a telephone call from the station that a man with a knife had gone berserk in a pub called the Dark Lantern, off the Market Square. I made steps (slowly) to the location to find all the customers had rapidly departed the pub and were outside in the street.

One customer told me that the man, who was still in the pub, would appear to be off his rocker. He looked at me as if he expected me to deal with this madman, I, on the other hand was thinking, Help! Hand on truncheon I entered to find the place apparently empty, then a head appeared from behind the bar. The bartender told me the man with the knife was in the toilet. Then the head vanished with some alacrity.

There was no back up in those days, no Support Group, Rapid Response Unit, Firearms Unit or Professional Siege Negotiators; in fact I was the only constable on duty in the whole of Aylesbury. The nearest assistance would be at Wendover, about ten miles away, but I had no means of communicating with them. It was up to me to deal with the incident.

I opened the door to the men's toilet to see the man standing there, on seeing me he started screaming and waving a big knife about. He went berserk and was making threatening moves towards me. I remember he called me the Gestapo and a member of the KGB.

Then suddenly his mood changed, he calmed down and started to mumble. I took the opportunity to talk quietly to him, to be honest I cannot recall what I said to him. After a few minutes of quiet negotiations he did calm down and started to cry. I took the initiative and convinced him that I would not harm him and he then handed over the knife.

I arrested the man and I walked him to Aylesbury police station where enquiries revealed that he was a RAF man who was an alcoholic and who became violent when filled with booze.

He was handed over to the RAF Police (snowdrops) and that was the last I saw or heard of him. There was no court case or court martial, and of course no publicity. I suspect he probably finished up in a mental home.

I made a note in the incident book and this book is read on a daily basis by the sergeant, inspector and superintendent, but not one of them commented to me about the frightening situation I had been confronted with. Nothing appeared in the local papers, it was, as far as everyone else was concerned a non-event, but to me, it was something I will never forget.

On another occasion I faced a knife wielding man, this was just before midnight on a Christmas Eve in the late 1950's. I was working a 4:00 p.m. to midnight shift because of possible trouble with drunks.

As I walked under the Town Hall arch on my way off duty, I was confronted with a man holding a knife who had suddenly appeared out of the darkness.

He advanced screaming that he was going to kill

me. With truncheon drawn I was backing away when another man appeared, and stepped between me and the man wielding the knife. He hit him with an uppercut, putting him on the floor.

My saviour told me that the man was his brother who was so drunk he did not know what he was doing. He said that he would take him home and there would be no further trouble.

I had to consider the situation as it affected me. It was Christmas Eve; I was due to go off duty in a few minutes time when I would be driving to Gloucester to join my wife and her parents for the Christmas holiday. After the man had been disarmed a bit of discretion was exercised on the assurance that the man would be taken off the street, I let his brother take him home.

THE POLICE WHISTLE AND THE JET FIGHTER

What, you may wonder is the connection between a police whistle and jet fighters, well under certain circumstances the whistle could be of vital importance.

Early in my training one of the courses I went on was at Brize Norton airfield where we were introduced to a fighter aircraft and in particular the Martin Baker ejector seat fitted to the aircraft.

We were given instructions in the event of a crash landing how to extricate an unconscious pilot. Access had to be gained to the cockpit and the ejector seat rendered safe.

To a person who had not seen inside a cockpit of a fighter plane I can tell you there is a bewildering array of controls, wires and other stuff. The pilot is connected to an oxygen supply, radio and other bits and pieces.

The most important point brought home to us was that before we touched the pilot or anything else the ejector seat had to be rendered safe.

The pilot has two ejector seat releases, one over his head and the other between his legs, and if one of these were to be accidentally pulled the seat and pilot would be ejected a hundred and fifty feet into the air with death the ultimate result. Also there is very little chance that the intended rescuer would survive the impact as the seat shot up out of the plane. This was a very deadly situation to be in.

This is where the whistle comes in. The hook at the end of the whistle chain that hooks into the top tunic buttonhole is exactly the right size to insert into one of the two seers in the ejector seat and this would render it safe.

The position of these two seers was imprinted on my mind and even today I believe I would recognise them (providing modern technology has not altered things).

Although aware of the whistle chain's use in such an emergency I did not, fortunately, have to use this safety precaution during my service.

YOUNG LADIES AND STATUES

Just outside Aylesbury and on the A418 road there is Hartwell House, a fine country house with some beautiful treasures within. In the surrounding grounds there are a number of monuments and statues.

After being a stately home, it became a girl's finishing school for 14 to 18 year olds. It is now a hotel.

When I was at Aylesbury it was still a finishing school. The large number of nubile young girls attending there, attracted the attention of a some of the young studs from Aylesbury and elsewhere and this brewed up a lot of trouble. When this situation came to the notice of the principal she made a complaint to the police.

Officers were offered overtime pay to patrol the grounds during the evenings and early nights. This extra paid duty was eagerly taken up by the Aylesbury officers desirous of a bit of extra cash.

I volunteered for this duty and my offer was duly accepted. Whilst carrying out this duty one warm summers and moonlit evening, it was just getting dark, when the back door of the house burst open and half a dozen young girls, dressed only in bras and panties ran out and chased each other round and round the statues, screaming and shouting.

I froze, just like the statues around me, and then when the opportunity arose I quickly hid behind one of the real statues.

I hate to think what the girls would have done if they had come to my statue. I am sure they were unaware that police patrolled the grounds during the evenings, and they would have had a shock when one of the statues, of a policeman in uniform came to life.

It certainly brightened up what would have been a long and boring but somewhat profitable evening.

A VISIT BY THE PRIME MINISTER

Another extra paid duty was at Chequers, the country retreat of the Prime Minister. Money was short in those days and these paid duties were keenly sort after. Only once was I able to carry out a Chequers duty and this was in a sentry box, halfway between the gates and the house.

It was tedious and time dragged by as it was dark, there was nothing to do other than walk about a bit, sit in the sentry box and then walk around again.

In the early 1960's Harold Macmillan was Prime Minister and he was holding a party that night for obviously very important people and all the lights were ablaze in the house. No doubt they were also discussing important matters of state whilst they partook of a sumptuous banquet.

About 10:00 p.m. I was aware that someone was approaching my sentry box, hand on truncheon, I challenged the person to give his identity, it was Prime Minister Harold Macmillan himself.

He spent about ten minutes talking to me, asking questions and even seeking advice about the state of the country at that time. He was a very amenable and friendly person who seemed to take a genuine interest in the police who protected him and his family.

Apparently it was his custom to visit the officers who were there to protect him. Perhaps he enjoyed their company more than that of his guests!

Unfortunately, I did not have the opportunity to act as guard inside the house with its obvious advantages. During the winter it is a lot warmer than a sentry box. Also, after the Prime Minister and guests had gone to bed, the staff, mainly WAAF girls from RAF Halton served up a delicious meal for the fortunate police officer on duty inside, whilst the man in the sentry box, if he was lucky, would get some sandwiches and a flask of coffee.

A VISIT BY THE QUEEN

During the late 1950's the Queen visited Aylesbury and I was nominated for motorcycle escort duty and it was one of those rare and proud occasions when all spruced up with the motorcycle highly polished, I was to ride in front of the procession as it made its way to the various places the Queen was to visit.

I am pleased to say the procession, in fact the whole royal visit, went off without a hitch.

TRAFFIC DEPARTMENT

Shortly after I had been transferred to the Traffic Division at Aylesbury in 1960 I was teamed up with Mel Lipscombe. He was ten years older than I was and an ex-paratrooper who had seen service during World War Two. He was also ten years more senior to me in the police service.

We got on well together and he gave me a lot of tips on advanced driving prior to my impending advanced driving course at Chelmsford.

TRAFFIC INITIATION

One day we were on patrol in our Jaguar along the A413 Aylesbury to Winslow road when we received a call to deal with some Gypsies who were encamped on private property.

It was my turn to deal with them on this

occasion. Stopping at the site where they were I took the usual steps, checked them and their vehicle's details, recorded the information in my pocket book and then gave them the twelve hour Gypsy warning, to move on or be prosecuted.

I returned to the patrol car and started to check the information over the radio to headquarters, when to my surprise, Mel got out of the car and he also went over to the Gypsies and checked their details, just as I had done. Did he think I was incapable of doing my job properly? I felt angry that he could not trust me with such a simple task.

As we drove off I told Mel in no uncertain terms that I was furious that he did not trust me to check out a few Gypsies.

Unrepentant and to make matters worse, Mel began to argue with me.

There was a frosty silence in the car for the next fifteen minutes or so, did I really want to work with such a person? Then, when we reached Winslow Mel asked me to stop in a lay-by.

He then said he had deliberately made me angry to see if my anger in any way affected the way I drove the patrol car. He was satisfied that my anger had not reflected my driving ability in any way so he would be pleased to have me permanently as his crew mate. We shook hands on it.

CARAVAN AND A BONFIRE

On another occasion we had an encounter with a Gypsy family. They had parked their caravan on a grass verge and not in a particularly good position. Parking on the grass verge was then an offence under the Highways Act as the verge is deemed to be part of the highway. We had to move this family on for their own safety.

Mel asked in the politest way for them to move along, but the head of the family, he may have been the equivalent of the Gypsy trade unionist, as he said he knew the law and refused to move on.

He said, "I know my rights, I have parked at this specific spot on the verge and this is where I am staying".

Mel did not say a word; he just walked off

towards Bicester and almost went out of sight. When he eventually returned he had a bundle of dried wood under his arm. Mel then placed the wood under the caravan.

Somewhat puzzled the Gypsy looked on, then when there was a tidy pile there, Mel got some paper and stuffed it under the wood, he then got out a box of matches and said to the Gypsy,

"If you say you have rights to stay at this specific spot, then I have rights to light a bonfire and roast some chestnuts at this specific spot. Do you want to move your caravan before or after I light my bonfire"?

The Gypsy moved pretty smartish. Of course Mel was bluffing but he had a polite but determined way about him that convinced the Gypsy he was not joking.

THE EXPERT DRIVER

About two months after joining the Traffic Department and with the driving advice from Mel, I was sent on a six week Advanced Driving

Course at Chelmsford, Essex.

This was a very intensive 'high speed' course that takes an extreme degree of concentration.

I was then about 27 years of age, had learnt to drive in a tank, passed my driving test in a 3 ton army lorry, had ridden motorcycles in competitions and been rallying my mini for a couple of years, so the course would be a piece of cake as I was an experienced driver. Or so I thought.

On the first day, those on the course were taken individually on a test drive. I went out with Sergeant (Galloping) Yallop, and after twenty miles of fairly high speed driving returned to the driving school, where the sergeant tore apart my driving ability. He even sat me in a dummy car and tried to teach me how to hold the steering wheel properly. My morale was shattered and I was very upset.

I was there to learn, so all those hurt feeling were put behind me and I buckled down to learn to drive the proper way.

There were usually three students and one instructor per car and the first car would go out at 9:00 a.m. on a designated route and five minutes later a second car would set out on the same route. The first car did not want to be caught up and the second car was hell bent on being first at the lunch stop.

There was no 70 mph speed limit in those days, and in any case police drivers on advanced driving courses were exempt from the speed limits. These were very 'high speed' drives.

Towards the end of the course we students wangled it so that I took over the wheel after the lunch break. I think it was some tribute to my driving as it seemed I was the smoothest and after lunch lulled the instructor to sleep, thereby giving us a bit of relief from his bawling and criticism.

One aspect of driving I had no trouble with was the skid pan. I loved every minute of it and had no trouble circling the pan in a controlled drift. Perhaps that rallying had come in useful after all.

I finished the six week course with a first class mark of 89, just two short of instructor level. I had learnt an awful lot about driving skills. I also learnt that anyone can drive fast; only a fully trained driver can drive fast and safe.

HARTWELL HOUSE AGAIN

We received a call to Hartwell House on another occasion. This was in the 1960's when I was a traffic officer.

The house had caught fire and my colleague and I spent several hours dragging furniture and other priceless objects out of the burning house and in the process got very dirty and inhaled a lot of smoke from the fire.

The house was quite badly damaged but we had managed to save probably thousands of pounds worth of priceless items. No thanks were received, just another part of police work carried out without recognition.

AN EMBARRASSING MOMENT

I started this book by mentioning some of the emotions a police officer will experience during his career. One I did not mention was embarrassment, an emotion that I was to suffer in plenty one sunny afternoon.

Mel and I had a call to attend an accident in Old Stoke Road, Aylesbury. Incidentally, my wife Gerry and I used to live in Stoke Road and this accident occurred about five hundred yards from our former home.

A motorcyclist had failed to negotiate a left hand bend, went across the road, through a garden fence and crashed into a tree.

We were quite near when the call came through and were there within minutes, even before the ambulance. A quick examination told us that the rider was dead. A nearby resident provided us with a blanket to cover the body.

I had to think about a post mortem, a report to the coroner and of course a coroner's inquest, so

I had to 'freeze the scene' and record every mark and piece of debris. Then the next of kin had to be informed.

As with all accidents there are always rubber-neckers, onlookers and the like who want to take a peek at the gruesome sight. We had to keep them back to preserve the scene.

One obtrusive onlooker was an Italian lad of about 23 years who appeared more pushy and inquisitive than the others, I had told him once to stand back, he did and then he came up to me again and tentatively asked,

"Is the rider alright",

I said to him in quite a brusque manner,

 "He's dead, now move back, I will not tell you again."

He seemed upset at this but I did not want him near the accident scene, I had enough to do recording the scene, taking measurements and tracing witnesses for the impending inquest.

He then blurted out,

"He is my younger brother."

Apparently he had recognised the motorcycle as

his own that the deceased rider, his brother, had borrowed earlier that day.

From being an obtrusive onlooker he would now be a witness as to his identity of the dead rider at the post mortem and at the upcoming inquest.

I deeply regretted the manner in which I had spoken to him bearing in mind the shock he must have received on my pronouncement. It was time to atone for my rudeness.

I placed him in the patrol car, consoled him the best I could and then took him to Stoke Mandeville Hospital, where he and his younger brother had worked as orderlies, and handed him into the care of the Almoner.

AN ELECTRIFYING THOUGHT

One night Mel and I were in Aylesbury police station and had just finished our late meal, it was about 2:00 a.m., when a lorry driver came in and he was in a state of shock.

He stammered out that he had just seen a UFO

between Wilstone Reservoir and Aston Clinton. Mel and I were sent out to investigate.

Needless to say nothing was found. After patrolling the road a couple of times we came to the conclusion that the lorry driver had seen his own headlights, in the rain, reflecting off an aluminium box at the top of an electricity pylon.

I do not know what Mel and I would have done if we had encountered men from another planet. Probably our Jaguar would have been extended to its utmost - in the opposite direction.

THE WOOD NYMPH

It was a lovely moonlight night, almost as light as day. Mel and I were driving past Wendover Woods when we saw a car parked on the side of the road. As the police had received several complaints of night time poachers in these woods we decided to investigate.

We followed a path into the woods and after a short distance came to a clearing. In the middle of the clearing, plainly visible in the moonlight were a couple engaged in, well, having fun. When they heard us approaching they broke apart, the man hastily got up and pulled up his trousers, but the young lady was not so hurried, she was completely unclothed.

It appears that when she undressed she had draped her clothes over the branches of several trees around the clearing.

Stark naked, slow and seductively she went to one branch, removed a shoe and placed it in the middle of the clearing, went to another tree and removed her bra and placed that in the middle of the clearing, then to another to collect another item, she so continued until all her items of clothing were together, then most provocatively she slowly got dressed. When fully clothed she said,

"Goodnight officers,"

Linked arms and with her friend, walked away, leaving behind two speechless and somewhat hot under the collar police officers.

It was not until they had gone that we realised that through the whole surreal episode not a word had been said by any of us until she bade us goodnight.

Incidentally, we never did find any poachers.

THE ABILITY TO READ

In the mid 1960s the Home Office in conjunction with a private company had developed a radar speed meter and the Buckinghamshire Constabulary were selected to try it out, I was one of the first officers in the force to use the radar for checking vehicle speeds.

After familiarization by the crews we put on a demonstration at Aston Clinton for all the magistrates who sat on the Aylesbury Bench. The equipment comprised of two big boxes, one contained the batteries and the other a monitor that emitted a ray across the road.

Whilst the magistrates watched the monitors, a patrol car passed the radar at exactly 30, 40, 50 and 60 mph, and the magistrates were impressed with the accuracy. Generally thereafter there were no problems with radar cases being proved in court.

However there was one man who pleaded not

guilty and after losing the case in the Magistrates Court went to the High Court on appeal. The defence counsel decided to call into question the accuracy of these machines. I was the first to give evidence, of stopping the offender and reporting him for the offence, and then it was my colleague Mel's turn to give evidence.

The defence counsel had made quite an issue about this new-fangled device, and how often they were checked for accuracy. He suggested that other objects, vehicles going in the opposite direction, even birds passing through the beam could have caused a false reading, etc.

Then the defence counsel asked Mel how the radar worked, Mel replied,

"I do not know."

The defence counsel, sensing a weakness and thereby success pulled himself up to his full height, put his thumbs in his gown as counsel usually do, and facing the jury said,

"Constable, you stand in the witness box, before the Judge and Jury, giving evidence on oath that my client was speeding based on a reading of a machine you were operating and you do not even know how the machine works?"

Mel said,

"That is correct sir."

This admission threw the counsel for a few moments, Mel then showed his wrist watch and said,

"I have a watch, I do not know how it works but I can tell the time."

There was no answer to that, the case was proved.

OCELOT SEAT COVERS AND WHISKY

Only once have I been asked to give false evidence in court and even today I feel angry and disgusted that a senior police officer could make such a suggestion.

During a tour of nights Mel and I were patrolling the A413 from Aylesbury to Amersham. Just south of the Great Missenden turn there is the Deep Mill Filling Station and opposite is a public house. It was about 4:00 a.m. and very dark, there were no street lamps or illumination from the only two buildings in the vicinity.

We pulled onto the filling station to check the security of the building and then saw parked behind it and in the corner of the parking area a Jaguar car. From previous visits we knew this car was not usually there and required investigation.

We got out and approached the car to find it was occupied by a woman sitting demurely in the front passenger seat. Whilst Mel questioned her as to what she was up to I checked the filling station and confirmed that it was secure.

The woman said that her male companion, the driver had gone into the bushes to relieve himself. She was not convincing so I went to the public house and woke the landlord, told him of the suspicious car and asked that he checked his premises for security. After doing so he stated that his premises were secure and nothing had been stolen.

I returned to the car. Meanwhile Mel had checked out the woman and the police records confirmed she was a well-known London prostitute who associated with London criminals.

Suspicions aroused, Mel checked the hedgerows in the vicinity but could not find the driver.

About ten minutes later a man walking along nonchalantly, arrived from a nearby field and in response to questions, particularly as to why he was so long away, it was now over half an hour, he said that he had been relieving himself.

Mel took him off to show where the dirty deed had taken place. Needless to say no such evidence was found. A check on the man indicated he was a petty London criminal.

With no apparent crime committed and after carrying out a thorough search of the car, its occupants and the surrounding area, and being satisfied of the couples identity and that they were not on the wanted list, we let them go. We had to accept that the man and women had been out in the country for a bit of heavy courting.

Before booking off duty that morning we made a full report and statements of the incident, just in case there were any future developments.

About 10:00 a.m. I was awoken from my slumbers with a request that I turned out and go post haste to Amersham police station in connection with the incident.

Mel and I arrived there about an hour later to be told by the CID that the landlord of the public house had found the trap door beside the pub had been forced and inside the cellar he found several bottles of whisky wrapped in an ocelot car seat cover. We had obviously disturbed the burglar when we drove onto the forecourt of the garage.

Enquiries were ongoing to locate the couple in London, meanwhile, the detective sergeant, I will not name him for obvious reasons, said that he had altered our statements and they just needed signing. Being a couple of canny coppers we declined to do so until the contents of the statements had been read and digested.

The detective sergeant had added to both our statements that when we checked the car during the early morning it was noted that the front passenger seat and the back seats were covered with ocelot covers but the driver's seat cover was missing. This was not so. Mel and I reached the same conclusion and refused to sign them.

Although agreeing with the detective sergeant that we were also convinced that the couple we checked that morning had been responsible for the break-in and attempted theft, we were not going to make a false statement and subsequently commit perjury.

We had to contend with an irate detective sergeant who tried, unsuccessfully, to pull rank on us, but we were adamant that we would not alter our statements.

The suspect couple were later arrested, charged and convicted, without us giving false evidence.

This was the first and last occasion during my thirty years in the police that I have come across a situation where a police officer has tried to encourage another to make a false statement and possibly commit perjury.

I remembered the oath of allegiance I took as a young recruit that I would serve without favour, malice or ill will and according to the law, and no one was going to make me do otherwise.

THE SERGEANT WHO LOST HIS FAMILY

Police officers do have time off and cultivate hobbies, and in 1960 I bought a brand new Mini Seven and this was used to quite good effect in rallies, driving tests and hill climbs.

To further my motoring activities, about the same time, myself and some others had formed the Buckinghamshire Constabulary Motor Club and we became one of the most successful police motor clubs in the country.

So much so that on four occasions (1962 to 1965) I was selected to represent the Federation of British Police Motor Clubs in the International Police Rallies held each year in Belgium, Holland, Luxemburg and France and we were loaned works rally cars by Ford and British Leyland.

Our motor club chairman was Sergeant Len Englefield, who later became a superintendent. He was a lovely man but had some odd traits for someone who attained so much in his police career.

I recall he had entered in the prestigious Midnight Rally being held in Wales. He entered his own car, a souped up Vauxhall VX490 that he wanted me to drive and he was to be the navigator.

We had not gone far before he suffered car sickness. And after two stops to enable him to get rid of his supper, I suggested we changed roles. I sat in the passenger seat and was fine, however, Len, even in the driver's seat, kept being sick. It was a disastrous night. He realised he was not cut out for this rallying lark.

This did not stop him from being a keen supporter of the club and one year he came over to Belgium to encourage our efforts in the international rally and on this occasion brought his family with him.

Len set up his tent beside the River Meuse near Namur, and left his wife and two children there. During the late evening he drove into Namur to meet up with the incoming rally cars at the first half hour stop and render what support he could.

After all the cars had departed the control about 2:00 a.m., Len headed back to join his family. Unfortunately, he had completely forgotten where he had left them and he spent several hours, until he ran out of petrol searching along the banks of the River Meuse.

In daylight he did manage to meet up with his family, much to his and his family's relief and to a lot of ribald comments from his colleagues.

THE STORY OF SIX PENGUINS

Whilst on traffic patrol I stopped a car and checked out the driver, and then whilst checking the boot I found it contained six penguins. I asked the driver why he was carrying them in his boot, and as he could not give a satisfactory explanation and did not know what to do with them, I said to him

"Take them to Whipsnade Zoo".

The very next day, I saw this car again, I stopped it, heard a noise from the boot and checked it and inside were the six penguins, all wearing sunglasses. I asked him what it was all about and he said,

"The penguins liked it so much at the zoo so today I decided to take them to the seaside".

NIGHTLY CHECKS

On many occasions in the days before the introduction of mobile phones, computers and even the telex system, these nightly checks have proved invaluable in tracking the movements of criminals and other ner do well's during the hours of darkness.

The Great Train Robbery took place at Bridego Bridge, near Cheddington, Buckinghamshire on the 8th August 1963. If the train robbers had passed through Aylesbury after the theft, there is no doubt they would have either been stopped by police, or their movement through the town would have been noted as the thieves were using a lorry and two Land Rovers disguised to look like they were Army vehicles.

There is no doubt the robbers had worked out a route using country lanes thereby avoiding towns and villages and meeting a police presence.

What a pity their careful planning was to no

avail. When the robbers left the scene of the crime at Bridego Bridge, they warned the Post Office staff not to move from the carriage for thirty minutes, or else.

This vital information indicated to the detectives dealing with the crime, that the robbers had probably gone to ground within a thirty mile radius of the scene of the crime. The detectives were right, the distance between Bridego Bridge and their lair at Leatherslade Farm, was 27 miles.

This leads me neatly onto the next story, The Great Train Robbery.

In 1963 the greatest crime ever to be committed in Great Britain occurred near Cheddington, Buckinghamshire: the Great Train Robbery occurred on my patch but at the time of its commission I was asleep in bed.

When I went on earlies later that day my involvement in this major crime was to be quite intensive for the next couple of years.

Frank Wright, a Detective Constable, as mentioned earlier the first constable in Aylesbury to own a car, who lived a couple of houses away from us in Priory Crescent was also on the investigation team. His wife Diana often called in to see us, mainly to brag how deeply involved her husband was in this major and sensational investigation.

When Leatherslade Farm, Brill, the lair of the criminals was found, an incident room was set up at Brill police station and Diana rushed into our house to tell us that 'her Frank' had the very important task of running this incident room. My wife and I were deeply impressed.

A week or so later whilst on traffic patrol I received a call to go to Brill police station where a sergeant told me to take charge of the incident room during the lunch period. I was flattered to be given such an important job, but all it involved was manning a telephone and recording messages from members of the public. Big deal.

I had delight in telling Diana that I also had the honour of running this very important communication centre in the Great Train Robbery incident room.

ALL THAT MONEY!

The Great Train Robbery was indeed the crime of the century. Up to that day in the summer of 1963 the sum of money stolen was the greatest theft in the world. The total amount was about two and a half million pounds. (Equivalent to £43m today.)

What is not so well known was that almost a third of the money was recovered by the police. Within weeks just under three quarters of a million pounds was recovered from the possession of the thieves and from other sources. So what happened to the recovered money? Well, there were a number of claimants, all demanding it was put in their hands.

The money, all used and worn notes, was being sent by the Bank of England from Glasgow to London where it was to be incinerated, so the Bank of England made a claim to it. It was being transported by the railway, and to cover their backs in case of a civil claim against the loss, the railways also made a claim. The money was being transported by the Post Office and it was in a Post Office carriage that on the night of the robbery was also a sorting office with about twenty of the post office staff carrying out their sorting duties. Obviously as it was stolen from under their noses they also claimed. Movement of the money was covered by insurance so the insurance company concerned also made a claim.

Confronted with these four claims Chief Constable Cheney told all the claimants that,

"I have the money and I am keeping it and if you want it you will all have to take me to court, sue me and make the appropriate claims."

The chief constable decided the money, that was then in a safe at Police Headquarters, Walton Grove, Aylesbury, should be in a more safer place so Mel and I were given the task of transporting it to the Bank of England in Threadneedle Street, London. We transported it in a prison van borrowed from the Metropolitan Police, with the money in the back together with a dog handler and his Alsatian.

On the way Mel and I discussed skipping London and carrying straight on, catching the boat at Dover, for France and continuing on to Spain where the money would provide us with a very comfortable living. It was all pie in the sky of course.

I did not hear what happened to the money in the end, I suspect the multiple claims were made in a London Court as nothing was published in the local papers.

Another way this robbery affected me personally was that on the day of the robbery it was to be the Force Sports Day, at Hazell's sports ground in Aylesbury, and I was scheduled to run in the mile. The event was cancelled. At least the crime did me a favour as I had not done any training for the race.

ESCORT DUTY

Another task that Mel and I were allocated was to escort the prisoners arrested in connection with the Great Train Robbery to and from Court.

At that time they were all lodged in Aylesbury prison. The building that was to become the new council office in Walton Street, Aylesbury, was hurriedly converted into a purpose built courthouse. This meant that we escorted them at 9:30 a.m., to the courthouse, back and forth from the courthouse to the prison at lunchtime, and then returned them again to the prison about 4:30 p.m..

During the three month trial period we got to know all the prisoners very well. Although there was generally a lot of grudging admiration by the public at the audacious way they executed the robbery, it should not be forgotten that they were a lot of hardened criminals and thugs who in the furtherance of the crime hit the train driver Jack Mills over the head and this severely affected him during the rest of his shortened life. They got what they deserved, thirty years behind bars.

THE NIGHT I LOST MY MATE!

Earlier I mentioned a fire at Hartwell House. Well this was not the only fire at a stately home we attended. A large house at Great Horwood caught fire one night, and like at Hartwell House we attended and helped to remove valuables from the burning building.

The fire had put the lights and telephone out of operation so we worked from the lights from the fire engines.

About 4:00 a.m. the fire was out, it was very dark, the fire brigade were about to leave and we had done all we could so also decided to leave. We were tired, dirty and hungry, looking forward to our well-deserved break.

Mel and I walked to the Jaguar patrol car that I had parked some two hundred yards away, I opened the driver's door and got in. I heard both doors close with that satisfying clunk that only expensive cars can make. I drove off but I soon noted that Mel was rather quiet, probably pondering over all the valuables we were unable to save, or more likely he had gone to sleep after our tiring removal job.

About twenty minutes later, as I was approaching Aylesbury and looking forward to a hot drink and something to eat, the radio broke into life, it was Headquarters requesting me to return to Horwood House to pick up my navigator. I called out,

"Mel?"

There was no reply, I put on the interior light, he was not there, or in the rear seats. I then realised Mel was not with me.

Apparently, Mel had remembered something as he was about to get in the car and had closed his door. He was then dismayed to see me vanishing down the driveway without him.

The fire engine had left, there was no telephone at the house so Mel had to walk to the nearest farm and wake up the farmer so he could use their telephone. As I drove up the driveway of Hartwell House I saw Mel at the top jumping up and down waving his fists, he was not a happy bunny when I picked him up, and I must admit I did feel somewhat embarrassed.

This was the second occasion Mel and I have been to fires at these huge houses and risked our lives, inhaled smoke and got ourselves filthy entering the burning buildings to recover someone else's valuables.

BLETCHLEY

THE WRONG TYPE OF OFFICER

In December 1966, I was posted to Bletchley, later to become Milton Keynes. Initially I was a beat officer but after a few months went back onto the traffic department.

There was a police officer at Bletchley called Coco Couling. Coco was not his real Christian name. I never knew what it was as he was always referred to as Coco, even by senior officers.

Coco got himself into financial trouble so he thought up a plan to alleviate his problem. Knowing how the police station worked, about 7am one morning he entered via the back of the police station and stole the typewriter from the charge room, took it to London and tried to sell it to a second-hand dealer.

The dealer was suspicious, probably because there was a 'property of the Buckinghamshire

Constabulary' sticker on the base of the typewriter and it had an extra-long carriage to accommodate the charge sheets.

The dealer, to allay his suspicions, told Coco that his clerk had gone to the bank for the day's petty cash and would not be back for an hour or so, and suggested Coco went to a local café for a coffee, and on his return the money would be ready. But before Coco left the dealer asked for his name and address. The fool gave his correct Bletchley address but gave a false name, Ron Lockwood.

Meanwhile, at Bletchley, the typewriter's disappearance was causing consternation. There were only four such machines in the station, the Superintendent secretary's, two in the typing pool and the one in the charge room. Initially the sergeant arranged a search of the premises, and then called in the inspector who called in the superintendent.

The extensive search of the police station to find the missing typewriter was abortive. It was inconceivable that someone would enter the police station and steal it! No-one had seen Coco take it and there were a lot of unhappy officers running round in circles.

Then the dealer telephoned Bletchley police station to check if the name and address given by Coco was genuine. The sergeant who took the call was Ron Lockwood. When the dealer said the seller's name was Ron Lockwood, things fell into place. Coco, the idiot, had given his own sergeant's name.

Following the phone call it was then realised the missing typewriter was in London, together with the culprit. A phone call was made to the Metropolitan Police and when Coco returned later that morning to collect his money he collected a pair of handcuffs instead, he was arrested. Charged and later convicted.

That was the end of Coco Couling's career in the police force. He must have been a right fool to think that he could get away with such a stupid act.

ALL LIT UP

Jack Barton, commonly called Dick Barton, special agent, was another officer at Bletchley who got himself into a bit of bother. He was one of the older officers and very near to retirement so was put out to grass. He was given a sort of country beat at Newton Longville, on the edge of Bletchley.

There is not much at Newton Longville, just a disused brick works and several streets. But the village did have some long fairly isolated lay-bys favoured by the local lads for a bit of courting

Jack must have missed the excitement of the town centre, so decided to get his thrills in another way.

Whilst on nights he revelled in upsetting courting couples who were snogging, or perhaps engaged in something more intimate, in cars parked in isolated places on his beat. He liked to see a bit of naked thigh or bosom. But his approach on foot sometimes alerted the occupants of the car.

To increase the element of surprise Jack decided to refine his approach. He decided to make his stealthy advance on his cycle. On seeing a car parked in a usual spot used by courting couples, Jack would remove his cycle lamp, hold it in his hand against his clothing so the light would not show and then would ride one handed towards the car, and shine the light into the side window hoping to see something exciting.

On the first occasion he tried his new approach, he saw a car in the moonlight parked in a quiet lay-by, the interior light was on, good, more illumination.

He, all excited, decided to have a peep, as is his wont he rapidly rode up but he misjudged his speed, course and distance, hit the back of the car with a crash, went over the handlebars, torch going one way, helmet the other, he landed on the roof then slid off into the roadway.

As the badly bruised and shaken officer staggered to his feet he was confronted by a married couple, who had been enjoying a fish and chip supper. Jack did not enjoy what was to come.

The occupants had received a nasty shock and Jack had a lot of explaining to do to them. The next morning, at the police station, he had to tell the superintendent how he had put a huge dent in the back of a car, and how the front wheel and forks of the station bike got buckled.

I understand he was a lot more circumspect during nights after this little incident and for thrills, well, he took up bowls.

THE BREATHALYSER

One warm sunny evening I was on a journey in the police van, an old Jowett, having picked up a stray dog, when in front of me I saw a car weaving all over the road. I stopped the driver and used a new handheld breathalyser on him, the result was positive.

I arrested the man and he was taken to Bletchley police station where the sergeant Ron Lockwood was unable to deal with the prisoner as he did not know how to proceed with the second part of the test, given the new breathalyser legislation.

On the previous day the new law had come into force and the breathalyser had been introduced for the first time into the British judicial system.

The prisoner was taken to Newport Pagnell police station where the duty inspector duly processed and charged the man, who was later convicted of drunk driving.

The poor dog meanwhile, still waiting in the back of the van, had a far longer journey to the canine rescue centre.

I can claim I was the first police office in the Buckinghamshire Constabulary to have used the breathalyser method to determine if a driver was over the legal limit.

MILTON KEYNES TRAFFIC

THE NORTHERNER

After a couple of months on the beat at Bletchley I was transferred onto the Traffic Department. The Traffic Department consisted of two sergeants and eight constables. We had two 3.4 Jaguars, and a Ford Zodiac estate car that was used mainly for motorway patrol.

I was teamed up with Geordie Formby, a forceful, dour character that originated from the north east of England.

I soon realised that Geordie liked the quiet life, he was also a scrounger. Our first tour of duty together started on a Monday night. Geordie took the wheel and made off quite smartly towards Woughton on the Green. I soon realised the reason for his alacrity.

In the village there was a fish and chip van. Geordie ordered two large portions of fish and chips and when I offered to pay for mine he told me that it was buckshee, he said the police never paid. I was reluctant to eat the food but I could not waste it.

It was the last time I 'used' this facility although it was Geordie's usual and first Monday night stop.

Geordie used to call into the Newport Pagnell Service Station and order a full meal that he never paid for, then, without asking he would fill up a large bag with buns and cakes to take home for his family.

The last straw came when we were at Newport Pagnell traffic office, and a man, shaking like a leaf, came in to report that he had been involved in an accident.

The story the driver related was that he was in the fast lane doing about 70 mph, overtaking some lorries when he was hit from behind by another, even faster motorist. The impact spun him round and knocked his car across two lanes in front of the lorries and onto the hard shoulder.

Fortunately the lorry drivers managed to avoid this luckless motorist and what could have been a very serious accident was averted. It could have resulted in a multiple fatal accident.

At least four drivers, including the lorry drivers stopped, gave the motorist their names and addresses and offered to make a statement to support any police action against the erring driver who they claimed had been driving dangerously and then failed to stop.

I had another matter to deal with and as it was Geordie's time to deal with the accident I left him to it.

When I returned to the office later, he told me in his usual smug way that he had talked the driver out of making a complaint. I was disgusted.

I immediately asked to be allocated another crew member and was subsequently teamed up with Ernie Drome.

THE ONE-LEGGED MAN AND A LOT OF SNOW

It was about 4:30 p.m. one winter's afternoon and Ernie and I were patrolling the M1. motorway near Newport Pagnell when there was a sudden and very heavy snowstorm, within a few minutes the carriageway was covered with two to three inches of snow.

The snow caused havoc with cars and lorries going off in all directions and there were several minor accidents.

Arrangements were being made to close the motorway but this always takes time. I had helped to move quite a lot of cars off the carriageway, and was so doing when I looked up to see a huge articulated lorry that had jack-knifed approaching me in what seemed a very fast speed. My speed matched it as I made my way up the embankment.

The lorry hit the central reservation gravel trap, the cab finished with the front up in the air and the trailer straddling all three carriageways. The driver was trapped and I heard him screaming. (He had badly injured his back.)

I ran towards the lorry and as I did so I saw another car approaching through the snow storm, wheels locked and heading straight towards the lorry whose trailer totally blocked the motorway, I knew that the occupants were liable to be very badly injured if not killed and if it passed under the trailer, the roof of the car would be ripped off and the occupants decapitated.

It crashed into the trailer with a loud bang, the doors flew open and four young men got out and scrambled up the embankment, two of them helping one of the others.

Fortunately, the car had hit the lorry's spare wheel suspended under the trailer and this had cushioned some of the impact.

I had to check the four men were o.k. I went to them and they appeared alright until one said,

"Will you get my leg out of the car?"

My stomach churned as I returned to the car, expecting to find gory bits of a body. To my relief all I found was a false leg.

With the help of the fire service the driver of the lorry, who had serious back injuries, was taken to hospital. Just another day in the life of a policeman.

THE COLOURED CONSTABLE!

Whilst on traffic duties at Milton Keynes I had a coloured friend called Trevor who worked for Blue Star Garages at the M1 Newport Pagnell Service Station.

Firstly I will digress a bit about the traffic policy as it was in the 1960's and how it is today as regards serious and multi-vehicle accidents.

In the 1960's after the removal of the dead and injured from the carriageway the first priority was clearing the motorway and getting the traffic moving. This is where the Blue Star Garage came in.

On receipt of information of a serious accident we would attend at the same time as the ambulance service. If there were trapped drivers, the fire service would also be asked to attend. Also called at the same time was the Blue Star Garage.

They would attend with sufficient breakdown vehicles to clear the road. Very quickly the dead and the injured were taken away, and immediately after that Blue Star Garage sprang into action. All the damaged vehicle were dragged, pushed, rolled or in some other way moved onto the hard shoulder and at least two lanes were opened to traffic, usually within half an hour of our arrival at the scene.

If prosecutions were demanded as a result of bad driving we always had sufficient evidence for the courts without all the modern aids, we did not even mark the location of the vehicles on the road with chalk.

Today (2013) when a serious, multiple or fatal accident occurs on a motorway, the police close the motorway trapping hundreds if not thousands of motorists and lorry drivers for several hours and I have heard reports of up to and over eight hours.

The police with their modern video and other recording instruments, accident scene investigators, vehicle examiners and scene of crime investigators carry out a thorough investigation. It would appear that a serious or fatal accident is now treated as a crime scene.

Meanwhile, the motorists are stuck behind the accident and they cannot proceed or go back.

They could be delivering vital hospital supplies, on his or her way to catch a plane, a business meeting, important hospital appointment or on a visit to a seriously ill relative, or for some other very urgent reason.

Every one of those trapped motorists had a reason, some of a very important nature, to be travelling along that motorway that day and the police have thwarted their intentions.

It is not for me to comment on modern day policing methods, but I do feel for those people trapped behind these accidents and wonder how they cope, with such things like the call of nature. I know which police procedure they would prefer.

Now back to my African friend Trevor. He was a lovely man, always cheerful, hardworking and a delight to be with.

One day we were walking through the lorry park at Newport Pagnell service station and he said to me,

"Brian, I am thinking about joining the police, what do you think?"

I considered his question, he was intelligent, had good initiative, presentable and I believe he would make a good officer, but in those days it was a rarity to see a coloured police officer. I said to him,

"You realise that if you joined the police you would become a Coonstable!

Trevor curled up with laughter and his infectious laughter soon had me going, and as we clung together, laughing, with tears running down our faces, we got a lot of bewildered looks from passing lorry drivers.

Trevor and I, in good fun, liked to call each other names and he often referred to me as a white honky (after a term used in the TV programme 'Love thy Neighbour'). 'You couldn't get away with this banter in today's culture'.

I do not know if Trevor did join the police as shortly after I was posted to Oxford on promotion and lost contact with him.

ONE FOOT LONG

Whilst on the Traffic Department I had dealt with many accidents in which motorists and motorcyclists had been seriously injured and killed, and after a period of time I had got used to seeing quite gruesome sights, but one such accident really sticks in my mind.

The story behind this accident was that a young couple who lived near Buckingham had a blazing row after the husband found that his wife was having an affair with another man. When the wife said that she was leaving with her new boy-friend, the husband said if she left him he would commit suicide.

About 9:30 a.m. the next morning, the husband got on his motorcycle and on a country lane between Gawcott and Buckingham swerved across the road and crashed head-on into a school bus. Fortunately, the bus had dropped off the school children and the driver was on his way back to the depot.

I was on solo patrol when I got the call to attend, I arrived as the body was being bagged up and the ambulance was about to take him to the mortuary.

I arranged for the smashed motorcycle to be collected and a relief driver to take away the coach as the coach driver was in such a state of shock.

Whilst waiting, I took a statement from the coach driver and he said that in his view the motorcyclist had ridden deliberately into his coach and he had been unable to take avoiding action.

After the coach and motorcycle had been cleared from the scene, I was doing some measurements and tidying up at the scene when I saw a boot on the side of the road; I picked it up and was really shocked to find the deceased motorcyclists foot inside.

This turned my stomach more than the sight of the dead body.

I put the boot (with the foot still inside) in the back of the police car and took it to the mortuary. On arrival I asked one of the mortuary attendants to remove it from the car boot as I felt too queasy to do it myself.

I later spoke to the new widow and she confirmed that her husband had the previous evening threatened to kill himself. It had been no idle threat.

FOUR AGAINST ONE

As a general rule there were always two crew members in a patrol car but occasionally illness, court duty or some other reason meant that you were on your own when an incident arose that required immediate action.

One such occasion was when I was driving along the A5 through Stony Stratford on my way back to Bletchley Police Station, I received a call over the radio that a driver had filled up his car with petrol in Bletchley and then driven off without paying. Within minutes I saw the car, a big Rover approaching me from the Bletchley direction.

I immediately turned round, sounded my siren but instead of stopping, the driver made off at fast speed towards Buckingham, I gave chase.

I saw that there were four men in the car. The driver was driving like a maniac and was a danger to other motorists. At least twice he mounted the grass verge and several other drivers had to take avoiding action.

Headquarters control monitored my calls in which I gave them directions as to the route followed by the driver of the other car. They tried to set up road blocks but we kept passing the locations before anything was arranged.

Fortunately, the other driver then left the main roads and stuck to minor roads, thereby lessening the possibility of a serious accident. Eventually he came unstuck, a narrow road they turned into ended in a farm yard and there was no way out. I now had to confront four desperate young men.

I got out, drew my truncheon, ran to their car, opened the driver's door and snatched the ignition keys. I then said,

"The first one out gets my truncheon over his head."

I stood at the front of the car with my truncheon raised.

Fortunately, no one took up the challenge and

they were still quietly sitting there when twenty minutes later reinforcements arrived and they were taken into custody.

What could have been a nasty situation ended peacefully. If they had taken me up on my challenge, and were armed in any way, it would have been a very one sided fight.

FROM FORCE TO FORCE

In mid-March 1968, I, a member of the Buckinghamshire Constabulary Traffic Department went on a driver refresher course at the Essex Police Headquarters, Chelmsford, Essex.

Whilst I was away, on the 1st April 1968, the Buckinghamshire Constabulary was amalgamated into the Thames Valley Police (along with Berkshire and Oxfordshire Constabularies, Reading Borough and Oxford City Police), so I came back as a Thames Valley Police officer.

A week prior to the 1st April the new uniform

jackets, helmets and insignias were issued to the 3,500 officers that then made up the new force.

As I was away I did not take delivery of my new uniform and on my return about the 14th April, the force tailor was so busy dealing with wrongly delivered, miss-fitting uniforms etc, I had a good excuse for not getting my new uniform, and for devilment I revelled in walking about in my Buckinghamshire uniform for another week or so.

I was challenged by several senior officers as to why I was not properly attired, but I had an excuse. Yes, I liked to be a bit of a rebel when the chance arose.

Looking back I believe this was the time that I ceased to be a police constable and became a police officer. I preferred to be known as a constable, perhaps I was a bit old fashioned.

OXFORD CITY POLICE

In March 1969 I was promoted sergeant, and much to my dismay posted to Oxford. I was a country copper, not a city slicker and I was worried I would not fit in. I had good reason to be concerned.

I remember the first day there, I had to see the superintendent who welcomed me to the station and then told me that contrary to what a lot of people thought, Oxford, the City of Sleeping Spires, was also a very violent place.

I was posted to A Relief and had a pretty good squad of fifteen men. I also had a good inspector in Doug Wynn.

The superintendent's words came true on my first shift of two until ten p.m. About 7:00 p.m. I had returned to the station (St Aldates) to relieve the station sergeant then shortly afterwards officers started to bring in prisoners. There had been a riot at a Chinese restaurant and seventeen people had been arrested.

It was my responsibility to decide in each case on the evidence provided, whether to accept or refuse the charges, remand to the cells, or to bail. Then to make out the charge sheets as appropriate and to deal with their property. It was a hectic six hours but it was a good initiation into the responsibilities of a station sergeant.

THE BERSERK DEMOLITION MAN

It was during a nightshift about six months after I had commenced duty at St Aldates that a major incident occurred. It started when a builder telephoned the station from a call box to say that he had strapped some sticks of gelignite to his torso and he was going to kill himself and his wife.

It was ascertained that he was a demolition contractor and was licensed to have explosives. He had discovered that his wife had been having an affair.

I sent an officer to the kiosk that he had telephoned from but he had gone, then within a few minutes he telephoned the police station again, from another kiosk repeating the threat. This pattern continued and all my men were running from kiosk to kiosk trying to find him. It was obvious he was unhinged.

Meanwhile the Cowley police had sent a man to his house in Littlemore, and because of the threat to her life removed his wife from the house and her neighbours from the house next door. Just after their doing so the deranged man arrived at his house. The officer tried to reason with him, but the man threatened to set off the explosives.

On advice over his radio the constable left the house and as he did so the man entered it and the house exploded. It was totally destroyed, as was the house next door.

Bits of the man were found and taken to the mortuary in St Aldates. No one else was hurt thanks to the prompt action of the police. I was glad to be on office duty that night.

THE ONE-LEGGED FIGHTER

One of my lads at St Aldates was Harry, a likeable Irishman who was an efficient officer although then somewhat short in service.

During nights we received a call from a public house at Kennington, that a drunken man was fighting anyone who got in his way. I despatched a car to deal with the incident. The crew then called for backup as the man was very violent, he had hit a couple of officers and they were having difficulty in subduing him.

Eventually he was overcome and brought to St Aldates police station and as station sergeant I had to deal with him.

Incredibly, he only had one good leg and it was amazing he had inflicted so much damage on the public and the police.

Whilst taking down his details he again became abusive and violent and it took a couple of officers to pin him against the wall. At this point our Harry, with his usual politeness and deference to authority, said to me,

"Excuse me sergeant, can I have your permission to 'tump' him"?

Needless to say, with some reluctance his request was denied.

Harry later became a detective sergeant and was an efficient anti-terrorist officer.

THE ENSENIOR PARADE

Shortly after my posting to Oxford I was called into the Superintendent's office at Oxford. He told me that I had, as the newest sergeant, been selected to lead the Ensenior Parade.

He told me that the parade was an old established custom where the entire senior Dons, Proctors and Chancellors of Oxford Universities, in their regalia walked from one college building to another, a distance of about half a mile. He also told me that it was a very slow procession as some of the older members were very doddery, and it was my responsibility to ensure none got left behind.

I duly presented myself at the appointed place at one of the colleges, dressed in my best uniform, shiny boots, helmet and white gloves.

The procession began, and the superintendent was right, it was a very slow dignified walk. After a short distance I looked behind and there were some stragglers so I changed my speed from slow to very slow.

Other officers held up the traffic as I and those following threaded our way from one place to the other. There was a big crowd watching the ceremony and I had a feeling of pride in the knowledge that I was leading a parade of so many famous and distinguished people. The procession ended at the Sheldonian Theatre where the Ensenior ceremony took place.

The superintendent also told me that as I was part of the procession it was expected of me at the end of the ceremony to lead them to St John's College where a reception was to take place and where I was to partake of the champagne, strawberries and cream and other delicacies that had been laid on.

I recall that one of the dignitaries on the parade was the 1st Earl of Stockton and ex-Prime Minister Harold Macmillan who I mentioned earlier. I reminded him that we had met before when I was on guard duty at Chequers. I recognised and spoke to quite a number of other famous people on that memorable day that included the former Home Secretary Roy Jenkins.

I am not a champagne drinker but had a small glass and enjoyed the exotic food that had been laid on. Generally, it had been a very enjoyable experience.

A BIT OF POLICE BRUTALITY!

I was on late duty one evening, driving the inspector's car in north Oxford when over the air there was a call that a man in a Rover had filled up with petrol at a garage in Oxford Road, Headington, failed to pay his bill, and to further upset the garage staff drove off with the petrol pipe still in his car's tank. The petrol pipe was torn from the pump and he drove off with it trailing behind. The car was a Rover so it was appropriate that it should have a tail!

I was driving along the Oxford Northern Bypass when I saw the Rover go past, complete with tail. After following the car for a short distance it was obvious the driver was drunk.

With both the siren and blue lights flashing, his befuddled brain was alerted to my presence and he stopped. I got out of the police car, yanked open the driver's door of the Rover, pulled out the ignition keys and asked the driver to get out as I proposed to breathalyse him. He refused to get out so with a bit of help from me, well perhaps a lot of help, he finally was outside the car.

On being told that he was under arrest for refusing to take the breath test he became awkward, grabbed hold of the top of the driver's door with both hands and would not let go. I prised his fingers open and got one hand off, put the handcuffs on, but he would then grip the door with his other hand.

I soon got fed up with him playing me about, so I withdrew my truncheon and by then he was holding the top of the door with both hands.

With a couple of sharp raps with my truncheon on his knuckles, he yelped a couple of times to coincide with the raps, he then let go, and in a trice he was fully handcuffed and in the back of the police car.

Was that a bit of police brutality or was it justifiable force necessary to execute the arrest? I will let the reader come to his own conclusions. I can say that he did not complain to the station sergeant about his badly bruised knuckles and he did not mention it in court.

At the Crown Court he was convicted of theft and drunk driving.

AT THE RIGHT PLACE AT THE RIGHT TIME

If you are in the right place at the right time circumstances can change your whole life. This happened to me whilst I was at St Aldates.

Although the work was challenging I was not entirely happy at Oxford. I had upset the other sergeants because I would go out on the streets and make arrests. The other sergeants kept reminding me I was a supervisory officer and did not do arrests and I should not rock the boat by making these arrests.

I was on earlies one Thursday in February 1969 and after my constables had been despatched onto their beats I went into the canteen for a cup of coffee. There was only one other officer in there that I recognised as a detective sergeant called Keith, so I sat at the same table.

I asked him what he did and he said he was in charge of the Motor Vehicle Investigation Squad that had been set up about a year previously. I did not realise there was such a squad and asked some more questions, meanwhile he asked me about my background and I told him I used to be a garage manager and a traffic officer, and that I had rallied and raced cars.

He did not say what he planned to do so unknown to me, he applied to Headquarters to go onto General CID and suggested that me, with my vast motor experience would be an ideal replacement on the Stolen Car Squad.

Apparently Keith's knowledge of motor vehicles was nil and this had caused him some embarrassment when dealing with suspect garages and motor orientated criminals. Especially as he was known as 'four door Mini Keith' after he had described one as such.

The next day I was called into the Superintendent's office and he told me that from the following Monday I would be transferred to Headquarters CID and take charge of the Motor Vehicle Investigation Squad, commonly called the Stolen Car Squad, based at Cumnor, Oxford.

From a police constable on the Traffic Department to detective sergeant in charge of my own department in just under a year! It must be some sort of record, particularly as I had not been CID trained.

I must add that when I took over the squad it consisted of just me and one detective constable, Don, but I generated enough work with good results, that soon after I had a squad of six, two at Aylesbury, two at Bracknell and two at Oxford.

CAR SQUAD

I am obviously biased but the Car Squad was an efficient unit and each and every year we recovered well over a million pounds worth of vehicles and arrested hundreds of criminals.

The squad became one of the most respected in the country and our services were used by other police forces, and I can recall working for Wiltshire, Gloucestershire, Northamptonshire and Bedfordshire Police. I even lectured to the Metropolitan Police.

As is my wont, I am a researcher and a collector of information so soon acquired a vast library of information about motor vehicles, caravans, plant equipment, boat specifications and associated information regarding documentation. Subsequently I was the author of several books on caravan, car and motorcycle identification, insurance, finance and hire purchase fraud and forgery of documents.

After attending lectures in the United States I became an expert in the investigation of auto arson on which I wrote an instruction book. I attended a couple of courses on boat theft and became proficient in that field of work as well. I also specialised in the field of insurance fraud.

DISAGREEABLE DON

When I inherited the Car Squad from Keith I also inherited Detective Constable Don. He was a bolshie so and so, small in stature he made up with cockiness. He was intelligent, but sly.

On my first day I noted in the diary that two days after I joined the Car Squad, we were scheduled to attend a CID meeting at Aylesbury. We duly arrived at the meeting in the gymnasium, Stoke Mandeville Hospital and I was surprised to see about fifty officers; from the rank of Detective Chief Superintendent downwards, who were in attendance. We sat at the back.

After an introductory talk by the boss, the inspector conducting the meeting called for the Car Squad to come forward. I followed Don down where he introduced me, Don then said,

"Detective Sergeant Brian Wood will now tell you about our terms of reference, about some recent cases and some of the tricks car thieves get up to."

This was totally unexpected and way beyond my capabilities and knowledge to respond at that time. My first two days in charge of the Car Squad were occupied in trying to understand my predecessor's filing system and to pick up the threads of his half investigated cases. Don had deliberately dropped me in it.

I simply explained to the meeting that with only two days in the job my talk would be very brief and that I wanted all the officers to know that there was a Car Squad for them to call on, and I would give them a fuller briefing at the next CID meeting.

Don, despite his efforts to embarrass his new

sergeant in front of so many people, then realised by trying to do so he had shown himself in a bad light.

Don also lived in Abingdon so we took it in turns to travel together to work. When it was my turn to drive I would pick him up at his house. One day he would get in and greet me heartily, chat all the way to work about anything, particularly his hobbies of stamp collecting and wine making. It made a pleasant change, because within a day or two he would get in the car, scrunch up in the seat, face the side window and not talk to me. This attitude would continue throughout the day and he would only speak if he had to. It was quite trying as he was so unpredictable.

On the other hand he was very knowledgeable about cars, lorries and motorcycles and was a good detective. On his good days as we travelled throughout the Thames Valley we would quiz each other about vehicle identification, police law and other matters that impinged on our specialist little squad.

I recall one day we had been to St Aldates police station in Oxford and as we left he was driving, turned into St Aldates and there standing on the pavement was the Chief Superintendent. For some inexplicable reason Don put the car in bottom gear floored the accelerator and drove in the low gear for about two hundred yards with the engine screaming at high revs. The Chief Superintendent stood there with his mouth open in amazement. I shouted to Don,

"What the bloody hell do you think you are doing, stop the car."

He drove round the corner and stopped, we got out, he then threw the keys at me, got in the passenger seat, went into one of his sulks and did not say a word for the next couple of days. I told him in no uncertain terms what I thought of him and his driving.

The Chief Superintendent did not call me in for an explanation, but this was not the end of the matter.

Don had driven us in from Abingdon on that day, and after work we left for home in his immaculate Austin Cambridge, his pride and joy.

Don sat in the driver's seat, with his overcoat on, collar turned up, and pork pie hat on his head, then off we went.

He always drove very sedately, never over 35 mph. As we approached Henwood village, I said to him, still rankled by his previous driving manner,

"Why don't you drive your own car the same abusive way as you do the police car."

To my surprise he suddenly accelerated up to about 50 mph, and as he approached a bend at Henwood, he hit the verge, lost control, the car swerved across the road twice before he managed to bring it under control. I really thought we were in for a crash big time. Thankfully, there was no other traffic about.

Don was really frightened by this experience and I must say he did moderate his driving of the police car after this little episode.

Don knew a German couple who he used to visit and they visited him. One day he told me the German couple were coming to England and suggested that we all meet up at the Conservative Club in Abingdon when he would introduce them to Gerry and I.

We were a bit late and as Gerry and I approached, he said,

"I bet you are late because you have been having a bit of nookey".

Needless to say this comment, made before two

total and foreign strangers embarrassed us both. It was the type of comment Don would make with the deliberate intention of causing embarrassment.

A few months later I received a package in the post, marked from Germany. It was addressed to me. Curious, I opened it to find inside a number of photographs of Don's German friends wife – posing full frontal, stark naked except for jack boots.

Shortly after Don asked me if I had received a package from Germany, I told him I had and asked why they had been posted to me? He then said that if the pornographic material was posted to him and was intercepted he could be in trouble.

I suppose he thought it was alright for his sergeant to get into trouble. A typical Don trick. I must admit however she had a lovely body.

About a year after I took over the Car Squad Don told me that he had passed his exams and was due to go on a promotion board. This put me in a quandary. To my mind a sergeant has to be reliable, steadfast, a person of integrity and fair-minded. Certainly not what moody Don was!

I was very tempted to put forward an adverse report to headquarters pointing out a few, well, quite a lot of factors that would show him in a bad light and that he was not fit to be a sergeant. If I did so, then I may have been lumbered with him for some time to come. In the end I kept quiet. He was promoted sergeant and moved onto traffic.

At the same time Jock and Dave came onto the Car Squad, at last I had a couple of good solid and reliable men to work with and I was glad to see the back of Don.

A couple of months later the squad was increased when we took on more men and opened offices at Aylesbury and Bracknell.

HORSES FOR COURSES

I am not a betting man other than an occasional Derby sweepstake organised at the various stations, but when you get what would appear to be a dead cert, temptation takes over.

It was during the steeplechase season that I was

at Didcot police station when a well known jockey called in to produce his driving documents following a routine stop. I was in the front office at the time and he gave the station sergeant the name of a horse. The sergeant in turn told me that the jockey's tips were generally spot on.

I should add that Didcot is the station that covers a lot of stables in the division and there was a good rapport between the stables, their wealthy owners and the police.

As we were in civilian clothes, Jock and I went into the nearby bookies and I placed a five pound bet each way on the horse. As at Ascot, it lost. That was the last time I placed a bet on a horse.

THE MAGIRUS DEUTZ CASE

As a result of a little bit of information we learnt that a small time haulage contractor had bought two Magirus Deutz tipper lorries on hire purchase for £40,000.00 each, and then he and the two lorries disappeared.

False information on the hire purchase forms indicated fraud so in effect he had stolen them from the finance company located in Wendover, Buckinghamshire.

We later found out that he had taken them up north and was working them on the new M180 motorway near Immingham. He and his driver were in digs there.

His driver got fed up with the long hours and was missing his wife and family so he packed in the job.

When the driver returned home to Wendover we were there to meet him. He told us exactly where the two lorries were, that they had been put on false plates, and even gave us the number of the one he had been using. It was time for us to pay a visit.

Dave and I drove up to Immingham and got ourselves some cheap lodgings.

Late that night we visited the partially completed motorway. There was a large port-a-cabin used as an office, another used as a canteen and alongside there was a large compound full of scrapers, diggers, rollers, JCB,s and a number of lorries. A flash of our warrant cards and the night-watchman let us in; we soon located the two lorries and identified them as the ones stolen by deception. A local recovery firm was called in to take the lorries into custody.

After a short sleep and early the next morning, dressed in donkey jackets, jeans and sweaters, we went to the port-a-cabin/cafe, and settled down with cups of coffee and bacon butties and mingled with the other workmen.

About 7:30 a.m. a man came in with a red face and breathing fire, claiming his two lorries had been stolen. There was a deathly silence, then I asked him what makes they were, he said "Magirus Deutz".

I then casually told him that I had them. He nearly blew his top. He came across towards me, I am sure he intended to tear my head off - until I slapped my warrant card on the table and said 'Police' - that stopped him in his tracks! He changed from a raging bull into a meek mouse in a nano-second. I then told him he was under arrest, he was then further deflated.

We took him to Hull Police Station where he was charged and bailed to Aylesbury Magistrates Court.

To celebrate a successful conclusion to the case and the eventual recovery of £80,000 worth of property, I made a decision that Dave and I would move into a nice guest house in Robin Hood's Bay, spend a day on the beach, partake of a nice fish and chip supper and have a good night's sleep, before we returned home.

The haulage contractor was eventually convicted for stealing the two lorries by deception and forgery of documents.

TO USE OR ABUSE POWER?

Police officers have an awful lot of powers, the power to detain and arrest, the power to seize, the power to enter premises, and many others. There is a thin line between exercising these powers properly and exceeding those powers.

On one occasion I used my position as a police officer to obtain a favour and this was under unusual circumstances and no-one was inconvenienced and no financial gain was obtained.

I was travelling to the United States where I was scheduled to lecture on European car crime at the annual conference of the International Association of Auto Theft Investigators in Houston, Texas.

My wife Gerry was accompanying me and we arrived at Gatwick airport about 8:30 a.m. for the 10:00 a.m. flight, and whilst checking in with American Airlines it was realised that Gerry did not have a visa to enter the United States.

On previous occasions Gerry and I had used our dual passport and the visa covered both, but a few months earlier Gerry had made a solo trip to Bruges, Belgium, and to do so she had obtained her own passport. It was Gerry's new passport that did not contain the visa and the book-in staff would not accept our dual passport.

A very helpful lady at American Airlines advised us to put our baggage into left luggage, catch the Gatwick Express to London and obtain a visa from the American Embassy; meanwhile she would see about getting us on a later plane.

We caught the Gatwick Express to Victoria, a taxi to the American Embassy, to be confronted with probably two hundred people waiting for visas. It was time for drastic action.

I found an American policeman, produced my warrant card and told him that I was to attend a police conference in Houston and the visa problem we had.

He took charge, he told Gerry to go downstairs and get two passport photographs from a machine there and he took us to the front of the queue, we had to ignore several comments from those already waiting. When Gerry and I got to the front of the hostile queue it would appear the circumstances had been explained to the clerk and the visa was quickly issued.

We took a taxi to Victoria and the Gatwick Express was just about to leave. We arrived back at Gatwick in less than two hours, to be met by the same lady from American Airlines.

After checking the visa we were expressed very quickly onto the 12:30 p.m. plane, and just to help us on our way that nice American Airlines lady had upgraded us to first class.

First class is the only way we can describe the staff of American Airlines and we used them as often as possible after this experience.

ASHES TO ASHES

So what sort of detective was I? Well, I certainly was not a Morse, Lewis, or even a Columbo. I did not always see the big picture, I could not envisage the end game of some intriguing plot, no, I was just a steady plodder. However, I plodded exceedingly well. When I arrested someone they stayed arrested. When I charged someone almost certainly they would be convicted. I made sure every avenue of the investigation had been explored and all the I's dotted and T's crossed before I submitted a report to the Prosecution Department. Let me give a little illustration.

I received a call that was thought to be about a car that had been burnt out in a remote location in the Chiltern Hills. When I got to the scene I saw just a car shaped area of ashes. The ashes were no more than a foot high, and at one end was the stub of an engine. I could not make out if it was a front or rear engine car, but the shape of the ashes suggested that it had been a car.

Obviously the car had had a fibreglass body – gone. The plastic number plates were gone and the alloy wheels had melted. From this I concluded it was probably a sports car, but what type? Identification seemed pretty hopeless.

In those days I was an avid reader of Arthur Upfield's books about the Aborigine Detective Inspector Napoleon Bonaparte. This detective would be called to the scene of unsolved murders that had occurred months or even years earlier. He would visit the scene and just sit there, studying the patterns made in the sand by the wind and made by ants and other creatures, and meditate – perhaps he was seeking divine guidance from the gods.

He would pick up some obscure clues and he always got his man. Would a bit of cogitation work for me? I decided to try it out.

It was a lovely sunny day, quiet and peaceful up in those woods; I sat on a fallen tree and deliberated, I thought about who the owner could be? How had the car got so deep into the woods, who set it alight, was it the owner in order to make a false insurance claim or a thief to obliterate his fingerprints?

Of course the supplying dealer would know what

registration number was put on the car and who was the first registered owner, but who were they? Where could it have been made, in England or abroad, the manufacturer would know, but who were they? So many questions and no answers. It would seem the answers had gone up in smoke.

As I sat there thinking about these matters, I then recalled that there were obscure regulations regarding the stamping of the chassis/VIN number, (Originally introduced by NHTSA, The National Highway Traffic Safety Administration in America and later introduced in the United Kingdom under the International Standards Organisation code number 3833), stipulating that the chassis VIN would be stamped on a part of the body that would not be damaged in a severe accident or destroyed by fire, so, under that heap of ash there should be a number.

Inspired by this thought I went to the police car and got my scraper, wire brush and cleaning solvent. Down on my knees I commenced digging among the ash I found a steel chassis. Starting at one end I cleaned the chassis and after about half an hour I found what I was looking for - a seventeen digit chassis/VIN number.

With reference to my VIN book I was able there and then to ascertain that it was a Lotus, the Elan model, made at Hethel, Norfolk, it had been fitted with a two litre engine, and it had right hand drive and was made in 1986.

I made a phone call to the Lotus factory and I found out the identity of the dealership to which the new Lotus had been supplied. The sales manager at the dealership informed me of the registration number.

At my request he checked the service history and this revealed that the car was in need of a very extensive renovation – it had been used for racing by the owner and had been crashed. The bodywork was badly split and the chassis knocked out of line. It would need about £3,000 worth of work to make it roadworthy again. I had learnt enough.

When I interviewed the owner, although he claimed the car had been stolen, I could prove otherwise.

His car was insured for use on the road but not on a race track so he could not claim to his insurance company for the cost of repair.

He eventually admitted it was his intention to report the car stolen and make a false insurance claim but had not at that time plucked up enough courage to report it stolen to the police and he had not notified his insurance company. So no false theft report had been made and no attempt made to defraud his insurance company. No criminal offences had been committed.

It is not a crime to burn your own property, but he had destroyed a vehicle that had some value, even if it was just suitable for spare parts. He did not get off scot free as I told the owner I would be informing the Forestry Commission of what he had done and they may charge him with the cost of removal of the remains of his car.

Cogitation can work, thank you Arthur Upfield.

THROWING A CASE

It is a police officer's task to obtain evidence about a crime and present it to the court in a proper and impartial fashion. There has been the occasional newspaper report of police officers fabricating evidence, concealing evidence, or in some other way assisting a defendant to evade conviction. Only once have I assisted a man to escape conviction and this was done in the interests of justice.

I went to see a woman who lived in Cowley, Oxford. She was a midwife who lived in her own house and took in lodgers. She had a very minor connection to a car theft I was dealing with and whilst I was talking to her she told me that she was about to report a crime to the police.

She then went on to tell me that she strongly suspected her lodger of stealing a diamond ring and matching earrings valued about £400 from her bedroom and that she suspected he had sold them as she knew he had money problems. She even suggested the name of the second-hand dealer where he may have sold them.

I took details of the jewellery and of the suspected man and promised to make the appropriate entry in the Cowley police station crime book.

Before doing so I decided to call at the second-hand shop in the Cowley Road and there the proprietor told me that a man fitting the description given of the lodger had indeed been in and sold the ring and earrings that day. The man had given his true name and the address where he was lodging.

I obtained a statement from the dealer and took possession of the jewellery, and later that day arrested the lodger.

The lodger stoutly denied theft and said that his landlady had given him the ring and earrings and requested that he sold them on her behalf and he had given her the money. In any event he was charged and bailed to the Magistrate's Court.

He pleaded not guilty and elected trial and in due course appeared at the Oxford Crown Court.

During the morning of the trial the midwife and the second-hand dealer gave their evidence and then the court adjourned for lunch so I went into the canteen at St Aldates police station to get a bite to eat.

A police officer, who had apparently heard about the case approached me and said that he personally knew the midwife and he also knew that about a year previously the midwife had made an allegation that her lodger had stolen a diamond ring and earrings and the lodger then sold them. We dug out the appropriate crime file and saw that as a result of her allegation the man had been convicted of the jewellery theft.

From the outset I had a very uneasy feeling about this case, although the midwife was very forceful about the allegation I had doubts about her story. Why would a man steal the jewellery from his own landlady and then give his correct name and address to the second-hand dealer?

When I returned to the court I told the prosecuting counsel of my suspicions. He agreed to my suggestion, and advised the defence counsel to ask me a certain line of questions when it was my turn to give evidence.

I entered the witness box, gave my evidence as required, then the defence counsel put questions to me that brought out the information about the previous allegation made against the previous lodger. At this point the judge ordered the trial to cease and the case was dismissed.

The judge also required the police to look further into this matter and I do know the midwife was later interviewed, but as I was not involved I do not know the final result of these further enquiries.

The midwife, following the alleged first theft had

made an insurance claim for the loss of the jewellery and had been paid out for its loss. She had not informed the insurance company that the court had made a restitution order, and the jewellery was returned to her, and it was the same jewellery that she, on the second occasion had made the false theft report to me.

PLAYING IT BY EAR

One of the most positive ways to identify a suspect is through DNA or his fingerprints, but there are other physical features that can also be used.

I had conducted an enquiry into the theft of a hire car from High Wycombe. A Pakistani gentleman had hired a car and in doing so had tendered forged documents and thereby obtained a nearly new car by deception. Further enquiries led me to believe the suspect had fled to his home country taking the car with him.

The only course of action I could take was to take out an arrest warrant and to circulate his name and description to all police forces. He had a previous conviction for the same type of offence so I had his photograph on file. Also his fingerprints would have been on record.

Several months later I received a telephone call from the High Wycombe police to say that the suspect had been arrested in London. I was not inclined to turn out as it was very late at night and on Christmas Eve and I had made certain social arrangements.

The High Wycombe police kindly arranged for the suspect to be transferred to their station and they would hold him in custody until the day after Boxing Day when I would go there to interview him.

He was interviewed by me as arranged on the 27th December and he proved to be a charming man and he told me he was a shop keeper in London and he produced certain evidence to confirm this. Nevertheless, he had the same name, the same date of birth as my suspect and originated from the same area in Pakistan and he looked very similar.

I could have taken his fingerprints and compared them with those on record but this would take time during this holiday period. There was an easier way; I checked his ears.

We all have different shaped ears and earlobes and this man's and the suspect's, as shown in the photograph, were vastly different. He was not the man I wanted.

I apologised and released the arrested man from custody.

Despite the fact that he, his family, and his business had been greatly inconvenienced and he had spent the Christmas period in a police cell. He apologised most profusely for any inconvenience he had caused the police. He was a real gentleman.

IT'S TIME TO ZIP IT UP

Only twice in the sixteen years I was in charge of the Stolen Vehicle Squad did I carry out duties other than dealing with motor vehicles. The first was a Department of Health and Social Security 'sting' at Oxford.

A couple of landlords in the Iffley Road had hit

upon the wheeze of selling rent books, duly made out and signed by them, to foreigners, layabouts, down and outs, etc, so that these undesirables could present themselves to the D.S.S. and obtain lodging allowances they were not entitled to as they did not live at the addresses.

This had been going on for quite a long time until someone at the D.S.S. realised that these three bedroom houses were each supposedly accommodating forty to fifty people.

An operations room was created adjacent to the D.S.S. office and six charge desks set up. I was in charge of one of these desks.

Arrangements were made that after signing in at the D.S.S. and collecting their rent money the claimants would be directed to another exit door, straight into the operations room and into the hands of the police.

The most vivid memory of that hot summer's day was that just prior to the operation beginning, knowing I was to be there for several hours, I went to the toilet to make myself comfortable, and then my fly zip jammed open. Try as I might it just would not close. To cover any possible embarrassment I put on my mackintosh, I was the only officer so attired.

During the course of that very hot day on which we processed some fifty fraudulent claimants, we were visited by several senior officers, bigwigs from the D.S.S and a local Member of Parliament, and my unusual attire drew a lot of quizzical looks.

I was very hot but at least I kept my dignity.

THE INCESTUOUS FATHER

The only other occasion when I performed a non-vehicle enquiry was when I was asked by the Oxford Duty Detective Inspector, as he was short of officers, to accompany a Woman Detective Sergeant on a delicate interview at a suspect's house.

Apparently the suspect had been committing incest with his twelve year old daughter. I am very pleased to say the interview was very successful, he was arrested and convicted.

I SHOULD NOT HAVE SAID THAT

Just a wrong word can have a profound effect on the outcome of a court case as was vividly brought home to me.

I had received some information that a man in Banbury, Oxfordshire, may have been in possession of a stolen car – a great boon to crime detection is a spurned girlfriend.

I went to the address given and quickly established that the suspect was indeed in possession of a car stolen from London. I arrested the man and confiscated the car. In a short statement he admitted its theft.

As the car was stolen from London it was a Metropolitan Police case so after a phone call, two officers from their C10 Department arrived and took away the prisoner and car. Case sorted.

I was surprised later, considering his admission of theft, to receive a witness notice to attend court at the Old Bailey in London and give evidence against the suspect. He had changed his plea to not guilty.

At the Old Bailey I gave my evidence that was simple and straightforward, or so I thought.

It is common knowledge that if a defence counsel has a tough case to defend, one of the best lines of questioning is to discredit the police evidence, making suggestions of planted evidence, statement taken under duress, undue force, violence and that sort of thing. This London defence barrister certainly tried it on with me and he made all sorts of spurious allegations.

In reply to one question, I started to answer him by saying,

"I suppose!"

I did not get any further. He pounced on these two words and turning to the Jury saying to them that supposition, not fact, was the whole basis of my evidence and all my evidence should be disregarded, and he continued in this vein in his final address to the jury. The case was thrown out and a guilty man had escaped his just punishment.

Apparently, the defendant's defence was that his old car was clapped out, a MOT failure and he was going to scrap it when a man he met in a pub offered to do it up for him and get it MOT tested for £100. This kind man took it away and when he brought it back a few days later, it had been repaired so good it ran like a different car. It fact it was a different car, another person's car.

The defendant then said that he now realised that this friend had changed his car for a stolen car and all the friend had done was swapped the number plates.

Obviously, the defendant did not know who he had entrusted with his car and £100. The money was paid in cash, he did not know his friends surname, where he lived or worked and had not seen him before or since. What a lot of cobblers!

A few days before this case came to court I had watched on the television a lecture by Sir Robert Mark, the then Metropolitan Police Commissioner, at the Lord Mayor of London's Banquet. He had made a powerful speech about crooked London lawyers who twisted the evidence, even concocted defences for criminals and who brought the legal system into disrepute.

When I left the court in a somewhat angry mood, I saw the defence barrister outside the court smoking a cigarette, I went to him and asked, "Did you see Sir Robert Mark's lecture a couple of nights ago?" he replied, "Yes," I then said, "Today I have met one of those crooked barristers he was talking about,"

I then walked off feeling a bit better.

THE MINER'S STRIKE

In the early 1980's the country suffered from a year long strike by the miners led by Arthur Scargill who protested at the closure of some mines by the then Prime Minister Margaret Thatcher.

The Thames Valley Police provided a large number of officers to police the demonstrations, and this meant that all of my officers were drafted on to the divisions to fill the gaps. This meant that I was the sole person on the Car Squad. I now had to do seven officers work.

I was working twelve to fourteen hours a day, and often at weekends. Despite the long hours the work piled up, and two months into the strike I forwarded a report to headquarters informing the bosses that I had a backlog of over

150 requests for help, most of which would result in the recovery of stolen property and the arrest of individuals.

The bosses replied; note up the files and forward them to the detective inspectors on the respective divisions/stations so they could allocate officers to take over the enquires. I knew this would not work but complied with the order.

When the strike was over, all my men came back, and so did about 80% of the jobs I had sent out to divisions.

Me and my men did an awful lot of overtime to get on top of the backlog.

Mentioning the miner's strike reminds me of a quote by another union leader, Eric Hammond of the Electrician's Union about the leader of the miner's strike, Arthur Scargill. After the strike was over, he said, "He started the miner's strike with a big union and a small house and ended the strike with a small union and a big house."

Quite cryptic I thought.

THE BIG TEXAN

In 1982 I attended a seminar at Houston, Texas, organised by the International Association of Auto Theft Investigators and I was scheduled to give a one hour lecture on the topic of auto crime in the European Economic Community (as it was then).

My wife Gerry and I arrived on the Saturday, this giving us a day and a bit to familiarise ourselves with the huge hotel and its surroundings. I also had a chance to meet a number of people I had met two years earlier at a seminar in Denver, Colorado.

One of the people I met at Denver then at Houston was a Texan police officer, he would stand out in any crowd as he was huge, about six feet four inches tall, about three feet wide. He also stood out as he was the only one in uniform and he wore it at all times (probably in bed) with not one but two holstered guns.

He seemed to get delight out of deriding my

country and would say,

"Hey Brian, I understand that Britain is so small that if you dropped it into Texas you would not find it again."

And,

"Is it right that if you drive in a straight line in any direction for more than fifty miles in little old England you finish up in the sea?"

And other such comments.

The seminar started on the Monday and I was dismayed to see that I was the first lecturer to speak after the opening addresses. There were over five hundred delegates in attendance, representing police, motor manufacturers, insurance companies, finance company, security, and many other bodies interested in auto crime.

The seminar was to be opened with speeches by a number of dignitaries, including the Governor of Texas, the Mayor of Houston, and the Chiefs of Houston Police and the Texas Highway Patrol, and some other high profile people. I knew from my previous experience that some of these would stay on to listen to the first lectures, and the first lecturer was little old me, a former country yokel and the first European to address this predominantly American event.

Those butterflies I had in my stomach felt more like an albatross by the end of the opening addresses.

I was called to the podium and after a quite embarrassing introduction, I looked out on a sea of people, all grim faced and forbidding. In the second row was that Texan, the only one with a grin on his face.

Then I had an inspired moment, I recalled something I had read in the 'Reader's Digest,' It seemed so appropriate that I started my speech with this impromptu anecdote. It went like this,

"Good morning ladies and gentlemen, it's great to be in the State of Texas. I understand Texas is the second largest State in America".

My Texan friend and others, probably also Texans, were nodding their heads in agreement. I went on,

"I recall the occasion when a Texas rancher visited an English farmer, and the following conversation took place",

"Say, how big is your spread"? Asked the rancher.

 The English farmer replied,

"From that clump of trees to the river over there, and from the back of the house to just over the ridge."

The Texan, somewhat disdainfully responded,

"Waal, my ranch is so big I get on my horse at sunup and ride and ride and ride, and by sundown I still haven't reached the end of my spread."

The English farmer said,

"I know what you mean. I've got a horse like that."

The audience erupted with laughter. Apparently most Americans generally do not like Texans who are always bragging about their state and it really set them off. I relaxed and the lecture went off a treat.

As a footnote, at the coffee break the Texan came up to me and stated,

"I saw you looking at me, It's the first time I have been put down like that,"

and he shook my hand and we became good friends.

The above little story reminds me of another

story about a Texan rancher, (Perhaps it was the same rancher). It goes like this:

A Texan rancher visited an Australian farmer. When the farmer showed him round his 1,000 acre farm, the Texan rancher said,

"Your little farm would get lost in my ranch".

The Australian farmer then showed his 1,000 head of cattle, to which the rancher said,

"I have ten times as many cattle on my ranch".

Then a kangaroo bounded past the couple, the rancher, the first time he had seen such an animal, said in astonishment,

"Good heavens, what was that,"

To which the Australian farmer said,

"Don't you have grasshoppers in Texas?"

THE LYON SEMINAR

On behalf of the International Association of Auto Theft Investigators, the European Branch held a seminar at the Interpol Headquarters in Lyon, France in 2001.   The President of IAATI and his wife came over from the United States.

During a social evening held by the Mayor of Lyon I was sitting next to the President's wife. In conversation she told me that this was her first trip to Europe and before coming over she had been reading up about Europe.   She then said to me,

"I understand that one of the European languages is Flemish, is that so?,"

I replied,

"Yes."

She then said,

"I have been studying a map of Europe and cannot find a country called Flem."

There was no satisfactory answer to that.

Historical note: Flemish is a Dutch language spoken by the people of Flanders, a region divided between Belgium, France and the Netherlands.

ARE YOU A THICKO?

One summer's day I was driving the Car Squad's unmarked Morris Minor 1000 traveller towards Aylesbury. As it was hot I had the 2/60 type air conditioning on, open both windows and driving at sixty miles per hour.

Between Milton and Thame I came across some road works controlled by temporary traffic lights that were at red so I stopped.

I saw a van with two young lads in it stop behind me. As first in the queue I could see the other end of the road works and watched as cars came through from the other direction. Then the opposite traffic lane stopped and the first car to stop flashed his lights to let me know his line had stopped and I could go through.

The lights facing me were still red so I remained where I was.   The driver of the van behind honked his horn, I ignored him. He then honked it again and I still ignored him, then he drove alongside me and stopped.   The passenger leaned out of the window and shouted,

"What's wrong with you mate, are you a thicko?"

I responded,

"No, I am a police officer."

I picked up my notebook and pen and said

"Are you going to be a thicko and go through?"

With some alacrity the driver engaged reverse and neatly parked his van behind my car. It was nice to see the change on their faces.

When the lights changed to green, for devilment I drove off at a sedate pace and the van driver kept a very respectable distance behind me. Perhaps he did not want his registration number taken!

NEARLY AN INSURANCE FRAUD

On a Saturday morning during the summer of 1983 a Pakistani gentleman from Coventry visited Oxford market and then in the afternoon left to return home. As he passed Hopcroft Holt that is about halfway between Oxford and Banbury he noticed the brakes on his white Vauxhall Cavalier Club had begun to fade, then eventually they packed up completely. His car was brakeless. He stopped on the grass verge, walked back to the garage at Hopcroft Holt to see if a mechanic was on duty. No such luck, so securing his car he hitched a lift back to Coventry.

The next day, with a friend who was a mechanic they returned to Hopcroft Holt to discover his car was no longer there – it had been stolen. The theft of the car was reported to Banbury police.

On the following Monday I had to go to Banbury on another matter, there I was approached by the constable who had taken the theft report, he was suspicious, who would steal a car without brakes? I agreed to look into the matter.

Shortly after I was approached by another constable who told me a report had just come in that a car had been burnt out in a side lane about half a mile from Hopcroft Holt, I said I would look at it on my way back to Oxford . It was going to be quite a busy day.

On my way back to Oxford I drove into the lane about half a mile from Hopcroft Holt where I found the shell of a car. I established it was a Vauxhall Cavalier Club and from the VIN that it was indeed the same one as reported stolen by the Pakistani gentleman.

I also learnt a lot more about the car as a result of my examination. I ascertained the fire had been set deliberately by using an accelerant. The heat had caused the roof to cave in and all the glass had melted. I found that the quite intense fire was started in both the front and back seats. All the manually operated windows had been wound down except one prior to the fire as indicated by the position of the winding mechanism. A wheel nut was missing from the front right wheel.

As my usual procedure I searched the debris under the steering lock and found just the ignition key. In a fire the ignition lock, usually made of aluminium and/or plastic often burns away and the key made of metal falls to the floor, just where I found it. The number plates, made of plastic had gone.

I searched the hedgerows and fields on the way back to the main road and found a red plastic petrol can in a field.

I then continued my walk to the main road and back towards Hopcroft Holt where there is a well-known public house and a small garage/filling station.

On the way I saw tyre marks on the grass verge where a car had been driven on and off the verge, I also found in the right track marks some fluid that looked and smelt like brake fluid, plus one wheel nut.

I visited the filling station where I showed the attendant the red petrol can and he confirmed it was identical to those they sold, and in fact, he told me he had sold one the previous day to a Pakistani, who was accompanied by another Pakistani.

He further added that the first Pakistani, then on his own had called at the garage on the Saturday enquiring if they had a mechanic on duty as his brakes had failed. I had heard and learnt enough.

I telephoned the car's owner and told him I had good and bad news for him about his car and arranged to meet him at Banbury police station on the Wednesday.

At the interview I asked the gentleman to relate what had happened to his car and he told me the story he had related to the constable a few days earlier.

I then said that I would tell him my somewhat different story. I said that his story about what happened on the Saturday was the same as my story up to that point in time. It was then that our stories were vastly difference.

I told him that his car was still there on the Sunday, his friend had in fact looked at the brakes, could not affect a repair so replaced the front wheel but left off one wheel nut. I showed him the one I had found on the verge. I then said that on his second visit to the garage, this time with his friend, he bought a red plastic petrol can and a gallon of petrol (a guess), walked back to his car and then drove the car slowly as the brakes did not work, into the lane, wound down all the windows except the rear nearside one, removed all the keys other than the ignition key from the key bunch and left the ignition key in the ignition lock, poured petrol over the front and back seats, set the car alight, left the scene in his friend's car after tossing the petrol container over the hedge into a field.

I then produced the petrol can and asked if he wanted me to fingerprint it and him. He declined the offer.

He must have thought I had been sitting up a tree watching them.

I then asked him,

"Have you been to your broker to get a claim form so that you can get money from your insurance company?"

At this point he withdrew from his pocket a completed insurance claim form and said,

"You had better have this."

As the claim form had not been sent off there was no deception on the insurance company, so no crime had been committed, but I arrested the man and he was charged with wasting police time, he pleaded guilty and was heavily fined.

A VERY FAST MINI

One day I received anonymous information that a man at Didcot was in possession of a stolen Mini. Details were taken and we made our way to the address given, I was accompanied by one of my men, Jock.

Now I should explain that Jock is a big man who commanded attention wherever he went, always immaculately dressed, bespoke suit, white shirt with matching tie and handkerchief in the top pocket. He always wore a gold tiepin and matching cuff links. He was Mr Smooth.

He was always correct in his behaviour, but he had a little habit, he had a tendency to fiddle. When we were asked to look at a car he would get in it, fiddle with the lights, wipers and any other knob or lever he could find, and he would poke around in any nook and cranny.

As we stopped outside the house of the suspect in Didcot, I noted it was a semi-detached, we could see up the sloping driveway there were two wooden gates level with the back of the house, and these gates were closed. The drive continued on up to a garage at the top of the drive.

We saw the Mini in question parked in the garage, the bonnet was up and a man was leaning over the engine.

I stopped in the roadway opposite the driveway, we got out and walked up the sloping drive, through the gate, I closed the gate and I then spoke to the man. I made the introductions and told him the reason for our visit and that we proposed to carry out a detailed examination of the car.

I asked to see the documentation, meanwhile Jock started his examination of the vehicle's identity, well, he got in the driver's seat and started his usual fiddling act.

Whilst I was looking at the paperwork, I suddenly heard a loud roar, the car leapt out of the garage, with the bonnet still up, both the owner and I ran out of the way. The car hurtled down the drive with Jock at the wheel, crashed through the wooden gates, wood flying everywhere, struck the side of the house with a loud graunching sound, bounced off then careered into the neighbour's fence. It came to a stop a couple of feet away from the police car. Jock leaped out, glared at the car and shouted,

"Bloody hell, bloody hell."

His entire suave demeanour had completely vanished away. He then commenced to kick hell out of the car. I was aghast at what had happened, as was the owner.

Jock was shattered, so was the Mini. I told Jock to get in the police car whilst I sorted out the mess he had made.

Apparently the owner was working on the carburettor cable and the throttle was in the open position, and the car was in gear so when Jock switched on the ignition, it burst into life, hence the hurried exit from the garage.

Incidentally, the car was not stolen, and all the paperwork was in order.

Jock received a severe reprimand from a senior officer and some re-training. The owner received considerable compensation from the police for a broken gate and a written off car. The neighbour also got a brand new fence. This was not the best day in the life of the car squad.

HOW DID YOU DO THAT?

It would be reasonable to assume that after this experience Jock would have been cured of his fiddling habit, no way.

A constable on night duty in Newbury at 4:00 a.m. one Saturday morning, stopped a man who was driving a Ford Cortina without a number plate, the driver was subsequently arrested for drunk driving, and for driving the car without number plates.

The car was taken to Newbury police station where their 'vehicle examiner' looked at it but could not determine its identity or establish if it was stolen, so the experts were called in.

Jock and I duly arrived and were appraised of the situation. I commenced the examination of the car and Jock, as usual, got in the driver's seat and started to fiddle with the controls. A few minutes later he got out and ambled off and into the police station.

Meanwhile, myself, the sergeant, with his hands

covered in oil was working under the bonnet collecting identifying features, being watched by the arresting officer and the 'vehicle examiner'.

Ten minutes or so later Jock came back and joined the other two men watching me, then one of the officers asked me,

"Do you think you will be able to establish its identity?

Before I could reply, Jock casually announced to the two officers who were watching my examination;

"The car registration number is so and so, it was stolen from 15 Winchester Street, Basingstoke between 10:30 p.m. last night and 4:30 a.m. this morning, the loser Mr Stephen Jones is on his way here, with replacement number plates, to confirm its identity and make a statement concerning its theft".

The two officers looked nonplussed, then Jock declared,

"The theft has been reported to Basingstoke police station, and the crime reference is so and so".

The officers jaws literally dropped and then they

wanted to know how Jock had identified the car without giving no more than a cursory glance at it, His comment,

"We are the experts."

And those bewildered officers, who were not enlightened as to how Jock had identified the car really did consider us to be the experts.

The loser, who sleeping late that morning had not realised his car had been stolen, later identified his car and the thief was convicted.

I can now reveal how Jock carried out this magical act. For some inexplicable reason Jock had checked inside the cowling over the steering column, found a bit of paper, palmed it and then went into the police station where he opened it up to discover it was a current tax disc for a Ford.

A quick check of the registration number on the tax disc with the Police National Computer revealed that the car had not been reported stolen but gave details of the owner.

Jock had telephoned the owner, who, due to late arousal from his sleep had not realised his car had been stolen until Jock told him it was at Newbury police station. Jock then telephoned

Basingstoke police station to report the theft on behalf of the owner.

Those officers at Newbury never did find out the true picture and I am still today bemused as to why Jock had to fiddle inside the steering column cowling.

There is a lesson to learn from this incident. Too many police officers check a suspect vehicle on the Police National Computer and if the computer shows no record of the car being stolen, this is taken as gospel. In this particular case, the owner, who had parked the car in his driveway overnight, had not realised it had been stolen until Jock telephoned him, and it was therefore not recorded on the Police National Computer.

I wonder how many stolen cars, being driven by the thief have been checked by the police but as it was not recorded as stolen at the time of the police check, have let a stolen car and its thief slip through their fingers?

ANOTHER AMAZING ACT

A car used by a thief working on the M4 motorway gave us another opportunity to baffle one of our colleagues.

Jock and I had been on enquiries in London and had finished early so on the way back decided to check along the M4 motorway, that was then being built between Maidenhead and Newbury, looking for suspect items of plant.

As we drove along the unmade road amid the diggers, scrapers, dumpers and tarmac machines I saw one of those marker posts that surveyors put up to mark the line of the road. Tied to the post was a set of number plates. I was a bit suspicious so made a note of their number and we then kept a look out for any vehicle minus plates, but we did not see anything suspicious that afternoon.

The next morning I carried out a check on the plates and discovered that the numbers related to a blue Ford Escort stolen from Meriden,

Birmingham a week earlier.

We were scheduled to do a further search of the M4 motorway road-works to try and trace the blue Escort, but before we left the office a call came in from a detective sergeant from Pangbourne police station informing us that during the night a constable had arrested a man for driving a car without number plates, the car was at Pangbourne police station awaiting our examination.

I told the officer that the car was the blue Ford Escort that had been stolen from Meriden, Birmingham, a week previously, gave him the crime reference number, and who the owner was and what the registration number should be.

There was silence from the other end of the line as the detective sergeant tried to digest this information, then the officer asked how I could provide its identity without even looking at the car minus number plates or not having the engine and chassis number. I told him we had our ways.

I then gave the officer the chassis (VIN) and engine number I had obtained from the stolen vehicle records and told him where to look on the car to find these numbers. He rang back a few minutes later to say that they matched.

That was another satisfied but bemused customer to add to our list.

A MISSED OPPORTUNITY

In the early 1970's there were a series of rapes in Oxford and surrounding areas and the team investigating these terrible crimes noted a number of similarities about the offender and his method of operation.

All five victims gave a similar but not very detailed description of both the man and his car. He told all of them that he worked away from home and returned to London late on the Friday afternoons. All the victims were picked up by the assailant on a Friday afternoon, usually in public houses, and taken to remote locations where they were raped and then tied to a fence or tree so that they could not make an early report of the crime.

The offender, once traced, would soon be identified by all the victims, but who was he?

Unable to trace the offender and wanting help to identify and trace the car, I was called in by the officer in charge.

At that time all that was known about the vehicle was it appeared to be a large car? I visited the scene of each of the five rapes and at the most recent one I was able to obtain some wheel marks and from these was able to obtain the tyre, wheelbase and track measurements. From the tyre impression in the mud I quickly ascertained the make and size of at least one tyre. It was a start.

Next I prepared a chart containing as many features about the vehicle as I could think of. Position of interior door handles, colour of the dashboard light, colour and impression of the bonnet size, bonnet emblem, width between the front seats, two of the victims had been forced between these seats into the back seat. Some thirty different features were charted.

Next I visited all the victims and questioned them in detail about the car in question and it was quite surprising what they could remember. When a victim was certain about a feature I marked it on the chart in red, when fairly certain in black and when there was a possibility it was marked in pencil.

Armed with this information I then knew the car was a big one and the wheelbase and track confirmed this. With this information I built up a profile of the car.

It was back to my office where my library of cars and their specifications and descriptions were perused and gradually by a system of elimination I was able to determine with some certainty the make and model of the car.

It was a Mark 2 Ford Granada. This information was passed on to the Rape Incident Room.

I believe this was the first time a vehicle identikit had been produced to help solve a crime.

In London, during the same period there had been a number of 'tower block rapes' and the Metropolitan police were zoning in on a suspect, but before his arrest he threw himself off of a tower block roof and died from his injuries. His description and photograph identified him as the Oxford rapist as well.

By the way, he owned a Mark 2 Ford Granada that exactly matched the description of my identikit.

As a postscript to this story, I had considered using my experience in this investigation to develop a vehicle identikit for all cars, to be used in solving future crimes. Before I got round to developing this, another officer from the Dorset Police, who, to while away the time whilst on a long stay in hospital, used motor manufacturers manuals to develop a vehicle identikit. This was published by his force and proved to be a successful tool in the detection of crime.

Another opportunity missed.

AIDING AND ABETTING

It is interesting to see the reactions of someone when they are embarrassed by being confronted by the police.

I recall in the early days of my time on the Stolen Vehicle Squad we had a call from Bletchley police to look at an old Austin Allegro that had been abandoned on a lay-by just outside the village of Shenley.

Jock and I arrived there, parked our unmarked Morris Minor traveller on the lay-by adjacent to the abandoned car.

So that we would hear any messages that may come over the police radio, we left the passenger door open.

Jock, in his usual way, was poking around inside the abandoned car; I opened the bonnet and was leaning on the wing and looking at the engine when I heard a car pull up. I looked up and saw it was an identical Austin Allegro to the abandoned car; a man got out and approached us. I resumed leaning on the front wing and continued looking for the engine number, trying to decide if I really wanted to get my hands covered in grease.

The man joined me, leant over the front wing beside me, in a chummy way he said,

"Anyfink worth stealing off of it mate?"

Before I could reply to his suggestion that I, a police sergeant, would assist him in a crime, the police car radio started to chatter, he got up, looked at me, then looked at Jock, who stood at a full 6' 3", and a look of horror came over his face as he realised we were police officers. Within seconds he was in his car and away.

Jock and I laughed so much neither of us thought to obtain the registration number of his car.

A VINTAGE ASTON MARTIN

Between Reading and Pangbourne there is a small industrial estate and on this estate, among other businesses used to be two small garages. One of the garage owners had a vintage Aston Martin that was in mint condition and quite rare and worth quite a lot of money.

The other garage owner coveted that car and had tried to buy it on a couple of occasions.

During the night the first garage was broken into and the Aston Martin was stolen. The distraught owner reported its theft to Reading police and due to the type and rarity of this car my squad was notified. Shortly afterwards the Aston Martin was found abandoned minus the doors, bonnet, wheels, cylinder head, battery, seats and several other easily removable parts.

Why would someone steal such a desirable car and strip it for parts that probably would not fit another car?

The distraught owner recovered his stripped car

and despite exhaustive enquiries with the Aston Martin factory and the Aston Martin Owner's Club and other sources he could not locate replacement parts. He was stuck with half a car.

But help was at hand, the other garage man, the one who had tried to buy it earlier, offered to take it off his hands and with reluctance, the owner sold what was left of his car at a knock down price.

Surprise, surprise, within a couple of months the new owner had managed to locate and fit all the bits that were missing and he finished up with a beautiful vintage Aston Martin. He had fulfilled his dream of owning that vintage car.

Criminals are, in my view, people with mental shortcomings and loose morals and this was so in the case of the stolen Aston Martin. The new owner of the Aston Martin, a married man, had a girl friend at Basingstoke, and as you might have guessed he had some connection with the theft of the car.

He had just ditched his girlfriend, perhaps she did not fit in with his new status as an Aston Martin owner?

A telephone call was received by the police from

this girl who had been ditched and she was full of spite and venom. The information filtered through to me and I interviewed her at her home and she made a beautiful detailed statement about the storage in her garage by her former boyfriend, the second garage man, of several parts of a car. She recalled seeing the Aston Martin emblem on some of the parts. All the parts described by her fitted those missing from the stolen Aston Martin.

Despite his knowledge of cars, what the thieving garage owner did not know was that all Aston Martin's are handmade and all major components are individually marked. For instance the last three digits of the chassis number (as it was then) are chalked behind the trim inside the doors and under the bonnet. Also the cylinder head was numbered.

The second motor dealer was visited, the car examined and the parts quickly identified as coming from the car in the first place. Arrested and charged, when he appeared at Reading Crown Court he pleaded guilty and was convicted.

CIA AGENT AT WORK

I have been called a lot of things during my police service, some good, some bad, but when I was called a CIA spy working for the U.S. government with a commission to murder someone I was quite stunned, even more so when this allegation was made in front of the judge and jury at Reading Crown Court by a man in the witness box giving evidence on oath.

This allegation arose after I had arrested the man for attempting to obtain £2,900 by criminal deception from his insurance company. It was a most bizarre case and to do full justice to it, I must give a fairly full account of how it came about.

I was on a routine visit to Aylesbury police station when a CID officer approached me and said he was dealing with the theft of a most unusual car, a Ford Mustang.

When he showed me the crime file I was more intrigued about the unusual circumstances than the unusual car.

The owner, a small time car dealer with a Walter Mitty personality, who I shall call John Howard, stated that one mid-afternoon he had driven the Mustang from his home in Tring, Hertfordshire to Aylesbury Market Square where it had broken down with a vapour lock in the carburettor. As he could not get it started he locked up the car, returned to Tring by bus to get his toolbox and then about an hour and a half later returned by bus to the Market Square to find the car had gone.

If the circumstances were correct it must have been a pretty smart thief to obtain access to such a rare car in a busy public place, have the means and know-how to start it, despite the fact that it had broken down and drive it away. I promised to make further enquiries.

At that time, traffic wardens were active in Aylesbury town centre which was liberally covered by double yellow lines. I located the warden working the market square that afternoon, and she assured me that no Ford Mustang had been parked during the pertinent times where the loser said he had left it. I visited the location from where it was stolen but there was no glass or other debris. More investigation was called for.

A check with the DVLA showed that the car was registered in the United Kingdom and Howard on acquisition had written to the DVLA stating that the car was a Ford Mustang and not a Ford Falcon as shown on the registration book.

Incredibly, and wrongly, the DVLA had amended their records and issued a new registration book without requiring the car to be examined.

The Ford Falcon was a low cost, low production model made in Canada and it was not very popular, whereas the Ford Mustang was a far superior car, a much sought after collector's car. They were vastly different and no way could the two be mixed up. The mystery deepened.

Through a contact in the United States I arranged for the car to be checked out and my contact confirmed the manufacturer's details and the chassis/VIN and engine numbers on the paper records did relate to a Ford Falcon, so Howard had given false information to the DVLA.

My American contact also advised me that the car had belonged to a US airman who had taken it to High Wycombe on his posting there. A DVLA check also showed it was last owned by a

US serviceman stationed at High Wycombe.

A visit to the USAF base at Booker, High Wycombe, revealed that the importing serviceman had recently returned to the United States, but I was fortunate to locate another serviceman who told me that he was aware that the car had broken down big time and it had been towed to a scrap yard in High Wycombe.

This was my next port of call and the scrap dealer in High Wycombe recalled taking the car in but as its engine was so completely shot he sold the car as scrap to another scrap dealer at Halton, near Wendover, not too far from where Howard lived.

The Scrap Yard at Halton was visited and I met the owner I had dealt with previously, a very violent anti-police Polish gentleman, but I got on alright with him and he was happy to talk to me.

He confirmed he had bought the car for a few pounds. He had taken out the broken engine and replaced it with a diesel engine out of a van and to do so he carried out a quite considerable conversion to match up the engine with the original gearbox.

He confirmed it was then a diesel engine Ford

Falcon and not petrol engine Ford Mustang. Furthermore, he had sold it together with the registration document and test certificate for £75 to a Mr Howard of Tring. It was time for an arrest to be made.

I went to his house in Tring where I initially met his wife who claimed she was a princess, a lie, and that her husband was a man of considerable substance and of high integrity.

Howard was arrested and at Aylesbury police station he was questioned but despite what I considered to be overwhelming evidence he insisted the car was a petrol engine Ford Mustang and it was stolen as stated. He was bailed so that I could make further enquiries.

One other facet that came to light at the time of arrest was that when we searched his BMW we found a revolver in the glove box that he did not have a firearm certificate for. This was handed over to the local CID but for some unknown reason he was not charged with that offence.

News of his arrest must have spread because I received a telephone call from a mechanic in Tring whom Howard had asked to fix the wipers on the car as they did not work.

I met the mechanic at Aylesbury police station and he made a statement including that he had worked on Howard's Ford Falcon of the number recorded, and that Howard had not paid him, hence his offer to help the police. He had test driven the car and confirmed it was a diesel engine Falcon.

I then visited all the garages in the Tring area and at a garage some five miles south of Tring I hit gold. I spoke to the petrol pump attendant and he confirmed that Howard had a fuel account with them and on several occasions he had filled the car in question with diesel and to back this up he showed me the accounts slips that showed the make and model, registration number and the amount of diesel that was put in the car.

The attendant also confirmed it was a diesel engine Ford Falcon. A statement was obtained and the diesel slips retained as evidence.

There was now sufficient evidence to take the case to court. He elected trial by jury and this was heard at Reading Crown Court. Four days were set aside for the trial.

The first problem in court was the Foreman of the Jury, he was a headmaster and on the very first day he had a row with the judge as he said he would not spend four days in court, but the judge put him in his place and threatened to imprison him for contempt of court, but despite this, from then on, this rather overpowering foreman showed his displeasure and complained at every opportunity.

The prosecution evidence went ahead without any serious hitches despite a lot of false allegations made against my witnesses.

When the defence started they produced two witnesses, one was a taxi driver who said that he had always wanted a Ford Mustang and when he heard this one was for sale he had viewed it, driven it and had almost bought it and he was emphatic the car was a petrol engine Mustang, and our prosecution barrister could not move him from this.

The next defence witness was a small time garage proprietor from Luton. Earlier Howard had said on oath that he had driven the Mustang down the M1 and near its junction with the A1081 near Luton it had broken down, also with a vapour lock. He had left it on the hard shoulder, walked one and a half miles along the motorway and at the intersection of the M1 and the A1081 there was a public telephone box that he used to call the garage. I knew all of this was rubbish.

The Luton garage man in evidence said he received the call, went to the M1 as indicated by Howard and loaded the vehicle onto his breakdown lorry and took it to his garage in Luton where he carried out the repair.

He produced a hand written numbered receipt allegedly for the tow-in and the repair and it was dated and appeared to be genuine.

This witness was a bit shaky on his evidence so I decided to do some checks. Firstly, on the M1, as on all motorways there are telephones a mile apart that are free and connected to the police control room, so why did Howard walk past one of these to find a public telephone box?

I contacted the Bedfordshire Police motorway control room and a search of the records confirmed that no telephone call had been made by Howard on the day in question. All the motorway telephones were in working order.

After the court adjourned that afternoon, I and one of my colleagues went to the location over the motorway near Luton from where Howard claimed he made a telephone call, no such public telephone boxes existed within five miles of this junction.

We then went to the garage in Luton; the garage owner who gave evidence was not there. After speaking to the mechanic, I then spoke on the telephone to the garage owner and told him we proposed to search his garage and seize any documents that the court may require, with or without a warrant, he reluctantly gave his permission.

The receipts were in a bit of a mess but what was abundantly clear was that the numbered one he had produced in court was completely out of sequence with the others and was a far more recent one than those made out about the time that Howard alleged he had broken down on the M1. We seized the lot.

The next day at court this additional evidence was produced, Howard could not have made the telephone call as there was no telephone box, he changed his mind and said he had called from the motorway phone, but this was quickly shot down on production of the police motorway log.

On production of the receipts from the garage the Jury were told to disregard the garage man's evidence.

It was whilst Howard was in the witness box that he said on oath, and to the surprise of all in the court, that whilst in the United States he had been engaged in gun running and when the CIA net was closing in he eluded them by leaving the country. He continued on to say that I, Detective Sergeant Brian Wood, an agent working for the CIA, had then been issued with a Walther PPK pistol and given instructions to assassinate him. Then he went on to describe in graphic detail how he had thwarted three attempts made by me on his life.

Howard added that because of the failed assassination attempts the CIA had changed tactics and instructed me to concoct the court case and get him put into prison, hence the present case.

When speaking about me from the witness box he referred to me as "my dear friend Brian". Other meaningless allegations were made about the police in general and he tried to convince the jury he was being persecuted.

Eventually, after a very eventful and lively trial the jury retired to consider the evidence.

I recall that whilst the jury were out I went into the toilet and there was the defence counsel; He said to me,

"You have won this one,"

I asked,

"Why do you say that?"

He replied,

"Well, he is as guilty as hell."

I then asked the defence counsel,

"If you believed he was guilty, why did you and Howard come up with such a cock and bull story and defend him so vigorously?"

He said,

"Money my dear boy, money".

He was right and wrong, Howard was guilty as hell but to the amazement of the whole court the jury found him not guilty. I wonder what influence that bolshie headmaster had on the other jury members that had an effect on the outcome of this trial!

In coming to their verdict the jury must have dismissed all the prosecution evidence, that of credible witnesses giving evidence on oath, documentation, all good and some of it of an official nature, and a very logical, provable and credible prosecution case, in favour of the defence case that could only be described as ridiculous to the extreme. No wonder the whole court was surprised by the jury's verdict.

At the records archives of the Crown Court at Reading, Berkshire, there is on file details of me, Detective Sergeant Brian Wood being a CIA agent who was supplied with a gun and ordered to assassinate Howard, and had failed. I do not know if I was upset the most by these allegations, or that I had failed on three separate occasions to bump off Howard!

I tried to get the garage man at Luton arrested for perjury, but I was overruled by our legal department.

Finally, that was not the last I heard about Howard, a few months later he went into a DSS office in London and tried to get benefit he was not entitled to. When he was refused he went berserk and later came back with a baseball bat, smashed the glass partition and set about beating up the woman clerk, for which he was arrested and charged and bailed.

Two weeks later Howard's body was found in the Wendover Woods with a shotgun alongside him.

I attended the inquest at Berkhampstead where the jury determined that he had committed suicide whilst his mind was disturbed. Did the jury come to the correct verdict? Did he actually shoot himself or had he been assassinated, possibly by a CIA agent?

JUST ONE LITTLE CLUE

Keen observation of a suspect person's reaction when he is being interviewed is part of the make-up of a good detective, or indeed of any police officer, as the following strange little story will illustrate.

One of my men, John, stationed at Aylesbury, had arrested a man for stealing two cars, putting them on false plates and then selling them to innocent purchasers. The evidence collected prior to the arrest was first class. It should have been an easy interview but despite the good evidence the man denied all knowledge of the theft of the cars.

I used to go to my Aylesbury office once a week and by design arrived about 12 midday. The timing was important, I spent thirty minutes checking my lads paperwork, then it was off to the canteen for ham, egg and chips for the next half hour, then it was thirty minutes on the snooker table, this was a vital anti-stress session!

On this particular day John's mate was otherwise engaged so he asked me to sit in on the interview with his prisoner. Due to a shortage of accommodation the interview took place in an empty office and the suspect sat on a table, the only furniture in the room, John and I stood against the wall by the door.

The suspect was a funny little man, very fidgety, foxy faced, so I will call him Freddy. We knew he had previous convictions for stealing cars.

John asked him some routine questions that he answered satisfactorily but when we got to the serious part about the stolen cars, Freddy emphatically denied any involvement in the thefts and subsequent sales, despite quite overwhelming information to the contrary. He was obviously lying.

During interviews, it is not just the reply to questions that is important, but the reactions of the suspects to the questions put to them, and their general demeanour.

My colleague had obviously noticed the reaction from Freddy during the questions so John quickly stepped towards the suspect, was he going to give Freddy a slap? No, John then knelt in front of him. Was he going to pray to him? No, John got hold of his ankles and held them firmly, was he going to yank him off the table onto the floor? No.

John then said something like this to Freddy,

"When I ask you a question and you give a truthful answer your ankles are not crossed, but when I ask a question and you lie you cross your ankles. I am now going to hold your ankles so that you cannot cross them therefore if you cannot cross them you will not be able to lie. Do you understand?"

He replied, "Yes".

John, whilst holding his ankles then asked him the same questions, and unbelievingly, the suspect without hesitation admitted the truth.

A statement was obtained from him admitting all the crimes. He was subsequently convicted at Court for the theft of the cars and deception over the sales.

Today the experts would say that John was doing a bit of criminal profiling or carrying out a study of body language. In those days we just called it a bit of good coppering.

IT WAS A DOG OF A CAR

In the mid 1980's I was asked by the British Broadcasting Corporation programme 'Nationwide' to do a short programme on stolen vehicles.

The outside broadcast took place at a military camp near Bicester, Oxfordshire, where the police rented a compound and we stored recovered stolen cars.

The programme concerned a 'ringing' gang that had used three cars in a complicated scam to hide the true identity of a stolen car.

The programme went off alright as the camera man followed me and the presenter around and I explained what had happened. It was a good experience.

About six months later Independent Television asked me to do a similar programme and this outside broadcast took place at Didcot, Oxon, again it went off successfully.

Later still, I was asked by Southern Television to do a spot on their current affairs programme, I believe it was called 'South Today.' This was to take place in the studios at Southampton.

I went to their studios where I met with the presenter Peter Clarke. He was a charming and laid back man and he explained that the photos I had brought with me would come up on a monitor and he was take me through the same complicated ringing scam step by step, as on the other two programmes. It would be a piece of cake; I was now an expert at this television lark.

We were in the same studio as other presenters and after the newsreader and the weather man had finished, Peter Clarke introduced me, then he started to talk about the stolen car, at this point, as advised beforehand, I looked at the monitor as I was to refer to the first car in the chain of three, and to my horror it showed a dog and not a car. I was, to put it mildly, somewhat flummoxed.

Peter was a true professional and despite the monitor then showing another dog, he took me through a somewhat shortened TV spot and it came to a successful conclusion. I, on the other hand was not feeling very comfortable, in fact I was distinctly uncomfortable and I did not think it was a very successful broadcast.

Apparently the next item on this current affairs programme was about the theft of dogs from the Southampton area and the member of the public who was to follow me into the hot seat was a dog owner who had suffered such a loss.

I hope by then they had sorted out the pictures and he was not confronted with the monitor showing stolen cars.

I am pleased to say I was not asked to go on any more television programmes.

THE COUNTRY YOKEL

It is surprising that even today there are still people who have not moved out of the immediate environment in which they were born. I came across such a person when my squad was conducting enquiries into the theft of a number of Kuboto tractor type machines from the Thames Valley area.

We had traced one to a place in Cornwall where it was examined but due to a fairly good piece of disguise work by the thief, who had removed all identifying features, a positive identification could not be made.

Through a process of elimination we were fairly certain that it belonged to a farmer just over the border in Warwickshire.

We saw the farmer and he told us that one of his farm workers had carried out repairs on the Kuboto and he was fairly sure the worker could identify his handiwork.

We spoke to the farm worker, let's call him Fred. He also thought he could identify the machinery but was reluctant to travel to Cornwall as he had only once or twice in his fifty something years travelled off the farm or further than the local village.

He had never married and obviously had a very sheltered life. We persuaded him to travel with us to Cornwall and lodging arrangements were made for the three of us at Marazion.

The first shock Fred suffered was when Jock travelled along a motorway at 70 mph. Tractor pace was Fred's only experience of speed.

He was a funny chap and he kept us amused with his comments about what he was seeing, it was as if he had been transported from the middle ages into the 1980's.

The hotel we were staying at in Mazarion did a good evening meal. I had stayed there a couple of times whilst on holiday.

When the waiter came to our table I ordered a steak and French fries. Fred decided he would also like a steak but he said to the waiter,

"I don't want French fries, I don't eat that foreign rubbish, can you do me chips?"

After the meal he asked if there were any ladies to be had in Marazian. I do not know what books he had been reading or even if he expected us to supply him with a lady as well as accommodation and food.

The next day we took him to the farm where the suspect Kuboto was and after he examined it we were beginning to believe we had wasted a lot of time, and money, then he took the battery out of its holder, and there was the date and his initials written in chalk on the bottom of the battery holder and obviously concealed by the battery. He had made a note of the date when he had fitted a new battery then added his initials.

This small but vital bit of evidence proved conclusive in the subsequent trial of the thief. Fred was not so daft after all.

AS PLAIN AS A PIKESTAFF

We quite often travelled outside the boundaries of the Thames Valley area. One reason was that a lot of the smaller police forces did not have a dedicated stolen car squad and our expertise was often called upon by other areas.

One such occasion was when we were asked to help Wiltshire police, at Swindon, who had unearthed a nest of car thieves and the police there had recovered thirty five suspect cars. My squad were asked to establish their identities and help with other enquiries.

The thieves had done a good job of disguising the identity of these cars, as where there was a possibility of badge engineering, that was what they had done. For instance an Austin Mini would become a Morris Mini; a Singer Vogue would become a Hillman Minx. (We are going back a long time now as you will realise by the type of vehicles I am referring to).

During, and after the identification had taken place, arrests were made, but one suspect had proved quite elusive to trace. To help with the outstanding enquiries and arrests we secured the help of the Regional Crime Squad from Bristol, and Detective Sergeant Stuart Smith of that squad was teamed up with me.

He was a good copper but alas a very heavy drinker when off duty. Despite this he was always sober in the morning, even after a heavy drinking binge.

On one occasion we had to go to London to do some observations on an address where one of the suspects lived. Stuart had acquired a Mercedes car from a local dealer and you would have thought that, in plain and casual clothes, and in that type of car we would truly be incognito. Stuart parked up a short distance from the suspects house and observation began.

About two hours into the stint, there was a knock on the car window, it was an old and kindly lady. She said,

"You officers have been here some time now I thought you would like some tea and biscuits."

She then handed us a tray laden with goodies.

So much for plain clothes! The suspect was not found that day.

AN OFFICER WITH A LOT TO SAY

Each year the Association of Chief Police Officers hold the National Car Theft Conference at either New Scotland Yard or the Metropolitan Police Training Centre at Hendon. About two hundred persons attend these conferences, representing all the police forces in the United Kingdom, and some from other countries.

There is also a good sprinkling of delegates from the Home Office, the DVLA, insurance and finance institutions, auctions, motor manufacturers, and quite a lot of other VIPs.

One year I noted that on the agenda, among the high flying people who have a lot to say, one of the speakers was a police constable (Steve) from the Northampton Police. At that time Northamptonshire Police did not have a Stolen Car Squad, so all us experienced delegates wondered what the constable would have to say at such an important and rather technical crime conference.

What he had to say made a lot of delegates sit up and take notice.

On his own initiative the officer had made an arrangement with his Local Vehicle Registration Office that when a person came in to re-tax his car, the MOT certificate, if appropriate, would be photocopied without the owner knowing, and the copy put in a tray for the officer to check on a weekly basis.

I should point out that at this time, in the mid 1980's about a thousand blank test certificates were stolen monthly from MOT stations throughout the UK, some with garage MOT stamps, and these certificates were sold, usually in public houses but sometimes by garages not authorised to issue test certificates. These would fetch between £50 and £100 each. This was big money as a wad of 100 test certificates would be worth up to £10,000 to the thief.

The Northamptonshire officer checked the photocopied MOT's against the stolen lists and the result was staggering.

In a six month period he had detected over three hundred stolen test certificates. The follow up enquiries in the first three months meant that over 150 arrests had been made for theft, burglary, receiving, handling stolen goods, forgery, tendering forged instruments, using a vehicle on a road without the proper documentation, theft of vehicles and many other minor offences. That was an average of almost three arrests a week. And the scheme was still ongoing.

He may have been a constable working on his own initiative, but it was damn good police work and following his talk at the conference, this procedure was followed up by other police forces, including mine.

THE DAY I MET THE PRINCE

I was involved in an event that did not have any connection with the police. This was the 1981 International Year of the Disabled, an organisation that was held nationally for the disabled at Silverstone race circuit.

The Thames Valley Police Motor Club was actively engaged in the administration of this event. Together with two colleagues I was responsible for ensuring that the invalid cars/carriages were mechanically fit to be driven onto the circuit.

Prince Charles was the patron of this event and he stopped by to see us at work. I suppose it could be argued that I met with the Prince but we did not converse or shake hands so the claim is somewhat tenuous. Perhaps I could claim that I had rubbed shoulders with the Prince, but he didn't even know as he had his back to me.

After the event was over I assisted in collating the scoring and other administrative work.

The event was highly successful and well-advertised in the newspapers and on television. In some small way I had contributed to its success and received a small medal for my efforts.

THE RACING MOTORCYCLISTS

Whilst on the subject of Northamptonshire officers and Silverstone; the Silverstone motor racing circuit is dissected by the boundaries of Northamptonshire, Buckinghamshire, and Thames Valley police, who shared the policing at race meetings.

The previously mentioned Steve and a colleague later became a sort of unofficial Stolen Vehicle Squad so we used to meet up on race days and check the car parks for stolen cars and motorcycles. Obviously, we also spent some time watching the races.

One weekend whilst at home, I was watching the motor cycle racing on television and a lad described in the commentary as a butcher's assistant, came off and comprehensively smashed up his Yamaha LC250 cc motor bike. The next week, in the same race series there was this rider described as a butcher's assistant, again riding a Yamaha LC250 cc.

I should add that in this series, the Yamaha LC250 was a road going bike. That led me to think, it could be the same rider, was he sponsored or did he have a good source of bikes?

I had a good friend in Hamish Brown, the manager of Silverstone race circuit, I gave him a call and he expressed the opinion that there were probably a lot of stolen motorcycles in this series. He agreed that we should meet and work out a plan.

The outcome was agreed that myself and the two lads from the Cumnor office and the two from Northampton Police should attend the next meeting and do some checking.

Hamish Brown supplied us with a list of the riders, giving their bike details, racing numbers and their home addresses. We donned white coats and assumed the role of scrutineers. We then checked the bike's engine and frame numbers as they went through the scrutineering bays.

One or two riders queried why we were checking the numbers and our reason was that, or so we said, that some bikes had been swapped between scrutineering and the race and we were there to stop this form of cheating.

Altogether, we checked out 105 motorcycles prior to the racing. We then enjoyed watching the races for the rest of the day.

Our work was not done as on returning to our base at Kidlington my colleagues and I checked all the engine and frame numbers on the Police National Computer, and incredibly we had twenty five hits on stolen machines. Almost one out of every four was a stolen machine or was fitted with a stolen engine.

Telex messages were sent to the police in the areas where the riders lived and the outcome was a number of arrests were made and stolen bikes recovered. Unfortunately, there were no riders from my police area so we did not have the pleasure of 'feeling' a few collars.

At Derby, their Stolen Car Squad visited one of the rider's home, recovered two stolen Yamaha's used for racing and two big Honda motorcycles, four for the price of one.

NO ARRESTS – NO CRIMES

Now back to the National Stolen Vehicle Conferences at New Scotland Yard. After I left the police in 1986 I was still invited to these conferences as I was a delegate representing the International Association of Auto Theft Investigators.

After I had left the Thames Valley Police, for some inexplicable reason the powers that be disbanded the well respected and successful Stolen Vehicle Squad that I had run for sixteen years, so when I saw the Thames Valley Police were represented at the conference by one of their officers, a police constable, I decided to make contact with him.

At the lunch break we sat together. I asked him how he was enjoying the conference. He said that he did not understand what was going on as everyone was talking in code and about things he did not understand.

I asked him if he was interested in car theft and

when he replied in the negative I asked why he was at the conferences as his forces representative. He had no idea at all why he had been selected as he had no interest whatsoever in cars or their theft.

What on earth was the Thames Valley Police thinking about sending a beat officer with no CID experience to such an important conference, particularly, as he was not even car orientated.

He came from Milton Keynes so I commented that that city had a major car crime problem. His reply was,

"Not according to my superintendent, she tells us that if we do not arrest people for stealing cars we do not have a problem."

What a pathetic attitude.

IT'S NOT WHAT IT SEEMS

It does not matter how respectable a person or a business may seem there is always a possibility that they are on the fiddle, or even into heavy crime. Such was the case of a garage business at Bletchley. This town is now part of the City of Milton Keynes.

I had received information from a police constable at Bletchley that this garage had been using hire vehicles on false plates. I found this hard to believe as they had over one hundred cars and vans on the fleet and it was a well respected business with the Austin, Rover and Jaguar franchises. However my contact was quite insistent so we did some checks and all vehicles came back clean.

About six weeks later the same information came from the same source but this time it concerned the company cars and not the hire cars. By coincidence, I had received a complaint from a local magistrate that he believed a new Austin Allegro he had bought from the same garage was not new.

Examination of the Allegro showed that it had been manufactured eighteen months before it was registered and therefore there could be some substance to the complaint. I decided to carry out an in-depth investigation and this investigation commenced in the October.

This garage had eight top of the range Rover and

Jaguar cars on their fleet for use by the directors and managers.

After some discreet observations I identified them by the registration numbers displayed. All showed the same sticker on the windscreen, a 'Tax applied for' sticker on the company's headed notepaper. Through the manufacturers I ascertained the date of delivery of the cars to the garage in question and all were delivered a month or so previously.

Fortunately for me, the garage had limited parking space so most of the company cars I was interested in were during the day parked in a free car park about 100 yards from the garage and behind a row of shops so I could with comparative ease casually approach the cars and take note of the speedometer readings and other information as and when required without anyone from the garage seeing me.

Usually the managing director's car was parked at the garage among the cars for sale and on a number of occasions I would, like any customer, look at the cars for sale and then casually look at the M.D.'s car as well. I was never challenged.

This garage, in common with most garages with high volume sales, obtained as a concession block allocation of vehicle registration numbers from the local council, in this case the Luton Vehicle Registration Office. At the end of the registration year any registration numbers not used on the vehicles were returned to the VRO and became redundant.

If these cars were being used by the garage in Bletchley on unregistered plates I had to find a way to identify them. I obtained from the police garage at Kidlington some of the red sticky plastic tape used on the sides of police cars and from this cut out small designs, triangles, crescents, diamonds, squares, etc. Then when the opportunity arose I stuck these inside the outer driver's door handles of the suspect cars. They were invisible and could not be felt. But I could see they were there because I had a dentist's angled mirror that was ideal so that I could check these little markers.

Over a period of just under twelve months I visited Bletchley once or twice a week and kept observation on the cars and drivers, noted if possible, mileages, time and place where seen on the public roads, photographed the cars with a camera hidden in a briefcase, identified the drivers as employees of the garage, and confirmed the car's identities with my little mirror.

On one dark evening I was travelling back from Bletchley through Stoke Hammond and this took me past the house of the managing director. He lived in a detached house about a quarter of a mile from any other property, and as I went past I saw his Rover outside the house silhouetted against a lighted window. I decided to do a bit of snooping.

I parked the police car in a field gateway, crept up his drive, I got my torch out as I wanted to see if I could get an up-to-date speedometer reading, just as I reached the car, at that precise moment, the front door opened and a bright security light came on, flooding the drive and the car, the managing director came out and headed for his car. What do I do, stand up and bluff it out, but I had no reason to be there as far as he was concerned.

As I crouched down beside the car I had another dilemma, would he come round the front or the back of the car to the driver's side where I was crouching. As his footsteps on the gravel got nearer I took a chance and moved to the back of the car, I got it right, as he came round the front I was moving round the back.

He got in the car and drove off leaving me stooped down in the middle of his drive. It's a good job he did not look in his mirror, or his wife come out of the house, as I was brilliantly illuminated by the security light. I did not try this type of detective work again.

In my office I put up a wall chart with all the relevant features of the cars, details of the vehicle and number displayed, sighting, mileages, drivers etc and gradually the evidence built up and the chart got bigger and longer. All of this information was also recorded in my pocket book.

At the end of August when the suffix change came up all eight cars ceased to be seen at their usual haunts. I checked with the Luton taxation office and this confirmed that all eight registration numbers that had been displayed on the cars had been 'returned' to the office allegedly as not used.

On my next visit to Bletchley I saw a new 'fleet' of cars were being used by the directors and, surprise, surprise, they were also displaying 'tax applied for' stickers in the windscreen. The garage was going to continue their tax saving scam for another year.

Luton taxation office supplied me with a list of the block of new registration numbers issued to this garage.

From the 1st September, by using these new numbers I monitored the registration of all the Rover and Jaguar cars sold by the garage and gradually cars of the same description and colour were registered with different and newly allocated plates to members of the public, mainly by people of substance.

More information was recorded on my wall chart, new registration numbers and details of the new owner. It was time for me to make some visits.

I visited all of the new owners and with their consent checked the cars and fortunately in less than a week I identified through my little stickers all eight cars that had originally been used on the roads on what was now regarded as new plates.

All the cars speedometers had been zeroed and where appropriate new tyres fitted. According to my checks all of these cars had covered between eight and twelve thousand miles before they were sold so they were far from new, as believed by the owners prior to my visit.

The owners, who were somewhat upset or even irate, were advised not to contact the garage or talk to anyone about this matter until the next phase of the enquiry was put into place. Despite the fact they resented being cheated by the garage, all conformed to my request.

The next phase was the arrest of the managing director and the search of his garages.

I required two search warrants, one for the garage at Bletchley and one for the service and pre delivery check premises at Stoke Hammond. Who better to issue the warrants than the Austin Allegro owning magistrate who had made the earlier complaint!

In mid-September, I and three of my colleagues were at his garage one morning when the Managing Director arrived at 9:00 a.m., driving a different car with a 'Tax applied for' sticker in the windscreen. He was arrested and taken to Bletchley police station.

Before leaving the garage I told the managing director's secretary that I would leave two officers behind and under the conditions of the warrant they required all the documentation in relation to the eight cars, manufacturer's invoices, service records, sales records to the new owners and any other information they may have on file.

I told her there were two ways we could go about it. She could locate all the documents and hand them over, or my officers could turn the place upside down and it would take her a week to put things right. She cooperated.

During the interview the managing director Donald Cook emphatically denied all involvement with the deception but he could not satisfactorily answer the questions we put to him so it was in that respect successful.

I put him in the cell to think things over for a while.

The seizure of the garage's documentation had been most successful. Some records showed the cars had been in their workshops for minor work, replacement tyres and the mechanic had put the 'false' registration numbers and the car's mileage on the service records. All good evidence.

The second search warrant was executed at the garage at Stoke Hammond where the pre-delivery inspections were carried out. There we found all the old number plates from the eight cars, drilled and covered in dead flies.

A worker there made a statement in which she said that she, on the instructions of the managing director, removed the old plates and used them as a template to drill the holes in the new plates and then fitted them to the eight cars, then removed the 'tax applied for' sticker and put a current vehicle excise licence onto the windscreen.

Another mechanic confirmed and made a statement admitting on the instructions of the managing director, taking off the part worn tyres and carrying out an intensive valet service and turning back the speedometers. More good evidence had been collected.

I had one final bit of work to do before it went to court. I took the old number plates back to the new owners of the eight cars and matched them up to the new plates, the fixing holes in every case were an exact match.

The managing director was charged with a total of eighteen counts of deception, unlicensed use, using vehicles on false plates, etc.

At Northampton Crown Court the managing director pleaded not guilty and strenuously denied all the charges.

The prosecution case held up very well, despite intensive questioning by the defence counsel. My recollection was of standing in the witness box for one and a half days, and my hips hurting.

When the managing director gave evidence one of the platforms of his defence was that with digital speedometers it was impossible to zero them from the 9,384 that was recorded on his car at my last sighting, the mileage I claimed he had done on the Rover car he had been using. It seemed a good defence.

I wanted to dispute this so after leaving court I went to a Rover garage in Oxford and the service manager directed us to a mechanic who showed us how it was done. We borrowed the speedometer from the garage that was set, to my request, at a mileage referred to in court earlier that day, 9,384 miles.

At court the next morning the managing director had, by coincidence also brought with him a speedometer identical to the one we had. We kept ours hidden. He showed his to the court, to the judge, defence and prosecuting counsel and the jury and explained in detail there were no knobs to twiddle to zero it.

Then our counsel showed him our speedometer, asked him if it was the same as his and asked him to note the reading of 9,384. He agreed it was identical.

The usher handed our speedometer back to our prosecuting counsel who handed it to my colleague who within a minute or so had changed the mileage back to zero. The defendant was shattered to see his defence collapse round his ears.

He was found guilty on all charges and fined £30,000. I know he was also sued by eight irate former customers and the Allegro owning magistrate. This was a very successful conclusion to a difficult case.

I must however give some credit to the defendant. After being found guilty he came up to me, shook my hand and complimented me on a well-researched and conducted investigation. This has never happened to me before or after.

Just a little thought. When I go to a restaurant and have a meal, a person, who perhaps I have never seen before or will not see again, takes my order, brings me my meal and then clears away the dirty plates. For this service that may take no more than ten minutes of their time, I am expected to tip, usually 10%.

In relation to the above related case, and in fact in respect of most of my cases, I would spend hundreds of hours on the investigation, sometimes working in my own time and at anti-social hours, recover thousands of pounds of property and open the door to allow the aggrieved persons to recoup thousands of pounds from the criminal who has stolen from or deceived them, or from their insurance company. My financial reward for all this work – Nil.

Wouldn't it be nice if I received say 10% return for the value of every car I recovered or for the large sums of money I have saved an insurance company? It will never happen of course because if police were rewarded for their work it would be open to abuse, and the police must be whiter than white.

DOGGONE IT!

On two occasions whilst performing my police duties, I have been attacked by dogs. I am not a lover of dogs but on the other hand I do not dislike them. Probably the best way to describe my attitude to these canines, is, that, when I have to, I tolerate them.

I had to see a man who lived near Slough who had reported his Ford Granada stolen. The reason his theft report had attracted my attention was that it fell into the category that suggested it may be a false theft report.

His elderly car had been left outside a pub one evening and when he came out it was missing. How many times have I heard, or seen this scenario at the scene of an alleged car theft?

I called by appointment at the man's house one morning and he answered the door. He was a very big man, about 6' 5" and probably weighed eighteen stone. Shaven headed and bulging with tattooed muscles. He looked quite formidable.

He invited me in and settled me at the dining room table and his wife kindly offered me a coffee. I spread out his documents on the table before me, driving licence, MOT certificate, registration document, certificate of insurance, etc.. I then got out my statement forms in preparation to taking a statement from him concerning the alleged theft, when his wife brought me a mug of hot coffee.

I had just started to sip the coffee when I was struck a violent body blow that knocked me clean out of the chair. No, it was not that brute of a man, I had been hit by a huge Rottweiler who had appeared from God knows where. The scalding hot coffee went everywhere, all over the papers, in my face; it soaked my shirt, jacket and trousers. I dropped the mug that smashed onto the floor.

The dog was not attacking me but was just over friendly so I cannot really claim I was attacked.

After profuse apologies from the couple attempts were made to soak up the excess and dry me out.

After the dog was locked away I took a rather soggy statement and concluded the enquiry and left to go home and get changed.

That was not the end of it, as the next day when I checked the MOT certificate, I ascertained it had been stolen from a nearby garage to where the man lived. Obviously, the Ford Granada was a MOT failure and in all probability my suspicion that the car had not been stolen was correct.

Initially I visited the MOT station from where the test certificates had been stolen and took a formal statement from the owner about the theft of the certificates.

I then made visits to the local MOT stations and soon found out where he had taken the car for MOT testing a few days before the alleged theft. The car had failed with a multitude of defects that would have cost more to put right than what the car was worth. Another statement was obtained.

This was just the right situation for a fraudulent insurance claim whereby the alleged loser hoped his insurance company would pay him out enough money to enable him to buy another car.

My next enquiry was at Drayton Scrap Yard, some five miles from where the alleged loser resided. There I located the alleged stolen Ford Granada, minus number plates. The scrap yard records showed that the owner had brought it in for scrapping a week or so prior to its alleged theft. I had enough information to justify another interview.

A few days later, with some apprehension, I made another visit to the man and his dog, and after ascertaining the Rottweiler had been securely locked away he invited me in. I confronted him with the facts I had discovered about the stolen MOT and to my surprise, he admitted all. He bought the MOT for £50 from 'a man in a pub', he had scrapped the car and it had not been stolen at all.

To sum up the interview he was as soft as they come and most apologetic.

I arrested and charged the man and he was later convicted with numerous offences including making a false insurance claim and handling a stolen test certificate.

A DOG WITH A BITE

On another occasion my encounter with a dog had a different outcome. I was looking for a man who was on the run and information came to light that he had been staying with a woman in Northampton. I had to see this woman.

By appointment one morning, I called at the address and she answered the door. She confirmed the wanted man had been there but had left a few weeks earlier. She did not know where he was at that time but knew where he was employed.

At that point a Jack Russell terrier ran out of the house, through my legs and scarpered up the road and out of sight. I was about to get my notebook and pen out of my pocket when, unknown to me the little blighter returned, leapt up and latched itself onto my left hand. It really did give me a sharp bite breaking the skin that necessitated a visit to Northampton hospital for treatment and a tetanus jab.

Ironically, the dog did not belong to the woman, but to her mother and she was looking after it for the day. It was just my luck to call on that particular day.

THE BIG AND SMALL OF IT

Jock used to relate a story about when he was on the Traffic Department prior to joining my Squad. He was teamed up with a man who was a bit scrawny and about 5' 8" tall. He was very different to Jock who was about 6' 3" and heavily built.

The smaller of them would sit at the wheel of the patrol car on a couple of cushions, wearing his greatcoat and would bulk himself out so that he looked like a tall and big man. Jock would slide down the passenger seat so that he nearly vanished out of sight in the foot well.

For a minor traffic infringement they would stop a motorist and as the police driver got out he would try to look as small as possible and when Jock got out he stretched himself to his full height. After dealing with the motorist, usually by caution, the driver would get back into the seat and resume his bulky stance, whilst Jock would almost vanish out of sight again in the foot well.

Apparently the officers got some pleasure in seeing the bewildered look on the motorists face. I suppose it was be a bit of light relief for them on a quiet day.

MURDER MOST FOUL

On a couple of occasions I have been called in to assist in both murder enquiries and terrorist attacks. One murder was that of Barry Page at Slough. He was a small time motor dealer who drove quite a posh car, if my memory has not completely failed me it was an Aston Martin.

He was shot to death in this car just outside Slough; it was a particularly nasty and gruesome murder.

Over the years Barry Page had imported into the UK a number of motor vehicles and it was thought that the motive for his murder was in connection with the importation of stolen vehicles.

An in-depth investigation was carried out by my squad into the history of the vehicles he had imported. None were recorded stolen or in any other way were they found to be illegal.

My investigation cleared away this possible motive therefore the murder squad could concentrate their efforts in looking for the true motive.

AND TERRORISM

During the IRA activities in the early 1980's a car bomb exploded in a car park at Heathrow Airport. Fortunately no-one was killed. This matter was dealt with by the Metropolitan Police Bomb Squad and the Anti-Terrorist Squad.

The car was well and truly blown to bits and its identification was causing some difficulties.

Eventually, a bit of metal with the chassis (VIN) number was found and it was established from this that the car had been a Morris, but which model and whom did it belong to?

But help was at hand. The explosion occurred late on a Friday evening and the Morris factory at Cowley, Oxford, was closed for the weekend. I was at home when the phone call came through and I was asked to help.

Fortunately, for the investigation team, my

contact at the Morris Factory was well known to me. I knew where he lived and even which local he visited on Friday evenings.

I soon located him, took him away from his pint and to the factory where we searched the records and located details of the vehicle that related to the chassis number of the blown up car.

Conveniently, the car had been supplied to a local dealer so I roused him from his slumbers and he was taken to his garage where the registration number and first owner details were ascertained from the garage records. This information was passed to the Metropolitan Anti-Terrorist Squad.

I had obtained this information within a couple of hours of the explosion, and as the car was not on the stolen records it was of vital importance. The last registered owner of the car had sold it to one of the IRA members and this early information assisted the police in effecting their arrest before they could flee the country, and the information was also vital to their subsequent conviction.

A DAY AT THE SEASIDE, AND BEYOND

My squad received information about the activities of a group of men from Pakistan then residing in Oxford. The evidence suggested they were buying cars on finance, usually large estate models, and putting down a minimum deposit then defaulting on the repayments. To further their nefarious aims they used false addresses and documents to evade paying the instalments. These cars were then to be driven to Pakistan where they would be sold,

I had been monitoring their activities and through the ferry bookings at Dover learnt of the day they were to be ferried across to France. My colleagues and I decided to arrange a reception party.

Jock, myself, and a Detective Sergeant from the force Criminal Intelligence Department went to Dover early on the scheduled day.

Just south of London we stopped at a café for some refreshments and the CID officer started to chat up the waitress and she was quite impressed. He, like Jock, was 6' 3" tall and smartly dressed. She tried to find out who we were and pulling her leg she was told that we arranged for people to disappear. At first she did not know what we were talking about, later it sunk in and she asked to see our guns!

At Dover we met up with our contacts from the Kent police and a Special Branch officer from New Scotland Yard and then laid in wait.

About midday a convoy of thirteen cars arrived, all driven by the Pakistanis. They were all arrested and lodged in the cells at Dover police station.

Then began the long task of sorting out the contents of the cars. All the cars were fully laden, with all sorts of goods. Some even had freezers, cookers, fridges on the roof. Inside there were smaller items like radios, toasters, kettles, bolts of cloth etc. A veritable Aladdin's cave of goods, all obtained fraudulently on hire purchase and as with the cars, a minimum deposit paid.

We spent the rest of the day and evening sorting out and cataloguing all the items; matching them up with hire purchase agreements and the people who had taken them out. It was quite a task.

About 10:00 p.m. we called it a day. As we had not eaten for some hours our Dover contact, the detective constable from the Metropolitan Police Special Branch who was on long term attachment to the Dover docks, arranged for a Chinese restaurant to stay open and provide us with a meal.

That was not the end of the day, I wanted a bed and no arrangements for accommodation had been made, but the other four wanted to have drinks. By then all the pubs were closed, so in two cars we set off from the restaurant, I did not know where we were going. I followed their car across town. We went up a ramp and finished up in the bowels of a cross-channel ferry. Our contact knew where there was an all-night bar!

Whilst at the bar I had my usual half a shandy and the others, being heavy drinkers, were well on the way to becoming blotto.

We were then approached by a little man, aged about thirty years, he had overheard our conversation and cheekily declared that we were police officers.

We invented occupations, I was a civilian photographer working on contract for the police, and the others told similar tales.

I asked this little man what he did and he said he was a jockey and produced his business card, James Morse, MA PHD. I commented that these were impressive qualifications for a jockey and he then explained that they meant Master of Alehouses, Public Houses and Distilleries.

Later he told us that he had married that day and was on his honeymoon and taking his bride to Paris. He then admitted that he had spent most of his money and only had twenty pounds left.

When asked where his bride was he pointed out a very unhappy lady sitting alone in the corner of the bar.

Our Dover contact, who knew the skipper of the ferry, arranged for the honeymoon couple to have a free cabin for the trip across to Calais. A sort of honeymoon suite.

I told the young lady the good news, she then said to me,

"No way will I be spending a night in a cabin with him, but if one of you would like to share it, that's all right".

No one took up her offer, or perhaps no one was in a fit state to do so.

A few minutes later I felt movement, we were leaving Dover. My first thought was, what would the Chief Constable say if he finds out that three of his men and one of his police car's was on an unauthorised trip to France.

We arrived at Calais about 4:00 a.m., and shortly after started the return journey. At least I did get a bit of kip on the homeward journey.

Our work at Dover was not complete, the Pakistanis had been in custody for almost twenty four hours and we knew that if they got bail we would never see them again so we collated a lot of evidence together and brought it and the men before the Dover Magistrates where we successfully requested for them all to be remanded in custody.

Then we had thirteen cars to deal with. Fortunately, the Dover Dock police had a large secure compound and we lodged them there until the finance companies could arrange for their removal.

Our second day at Dover also finished after 10 p.m. What we did afterwards is a bit hazy, but I do know that in the early hours we were at the Special Branch officer's house above Dover cliffs. He had a couple of bottles of whiskey that was being consumed quite rapidly. As a virtual non-drinker, I was asked by the S.B. man to take his two dogs for a walk.

To get away from the smoke and liquor laden atmosphere, I was quite happy to do so, until I saw the dogs. Those dogs were huge, I believe they were Dobermans.

With some difficulty I walked them on their leads for a couple of miles along the cliff tops, then when I was going through a gate I let go of one of the leads and promptly lost one of the dogs.

As I previously mentioned I do not particularly like dogs so what was I doing at 4:00 a.m. in the morning walking them in the dark along paths I did not know? I must have been mad.

I made my way back to the house and with relief I saw the missing dog had made its own way back. A short kip followed and then it was back to Oxford to finalise the case.

Ultimately, all the defendants were convicted and the property restored to the respective finance companies.

ARSON AND INSURANCE FRAUD

Arson and insurance fraud often go hand in hand and over the years with the Car Squad I have dealt with many car fires that have been set by the owner with a view to making a false insurance claim.

The reasons for these false claims have many backgrounds, failed MOT, heavy repair bills looming, hire purchase debt, and financial difficulties, etc.

I have specialised in auto arson and a lot of my knowledge was obtained from seminars in the United States where they were well ahead of the British police in both investigative techniques and forensic science. An in-depth examination of a burnt out shell of a car can reveal a lot of useful information.

I have already related one story about an attempted false insurance claim following a car fire; well there are many other reasons and means used by dishonest motorists who use

251

their transport with a view to extracting money from their insurance companies.

In the early 1980's, I used to have informal meetings with the claims managers of a number of insurance companies at Reading where I would inform them of the latest scams by these fraudsters, and in return I asked them to provide me with information if any unusual patterns arose in respect of insurance claims received.

As a result of these quarterly meetings I gleaned a lot of information, and one such information was that there were an unusually high number of insurance claims from motorists in Slough submitted by Asians.

I should stress that I am not in any way racist, but facts are facts and I am not being selective in referring just to one class of citizen.

At Slough, the stolen car records are computerised so if a car is stolen it is on the computer but when recovered the record is deleted. However, the office manager, Stan, as well as using the computers also maintained the old stolen vehicles register and this was what I was interested in.

Slough has a high incidence of car theft and these

were the centre of my attention. I checked the records in the old register of stolen and recovered vehicles and divided them into two classes, those reported stolen by owners with what would appear to be non-Asian names and those with Asian names.

I then compared the non-recovered vehicles and I found out that about 70% of non-Asian owned vehicles were recovered whilst only 20% of Asian owned vehicles were recovered. Why?

With a map of Slough, I looked at the locations where the Asian losers lived and came up with some remarkable figures, for instance, at 20 Northern Road, within a period of one year there had been thirteen vehicles stolen from people allegedly resident at that one house. Can you imagine, thirteen vehicles stolen from one householder? One a month. How many persons lived there?

Also ascertained, was that people who lived at that address would appear to have multiple names.

All the information was charted so the pattern of claims was made clear, and then with the assistance of the Slough CID, an operation was set up and a number of claimants arrested and subsequently convicted. There was then a marked decrease in the number of cars stolen in the Slough area.

THE CAR HIRE SCAM

A group of people at High Wycombe were making a lot of money by submitting false insurance claims in relation to staged accidents at High Wycombe, and like the Slough enquiry above, this information came from the insurance claims managers at Reading.

I had dealt with staged accidents before, when a person would brake suddenly and heavily, causing the car behind to crash into the back of the first driver's car. This is what was happening at High Wycombe. As a general rule if someone runs into the back of another car, the person so doing is held to be at fault.

In these cases, after the staged accident, usually at a roundabout, the driver and his passenger of the car crashed into would get out and complain of whiplash injuries. They would then claim on the other persons insurance for damage to their car and for their injuries.

These people were so proficient at running this system their claims were nearly always met and on average about £15,000 was extracted per claim from the insurance companies involved.

The downside was that the criminals own car suffered damage that had to be repaired, usually at the expense of the other driver's insurance company, so a refinement was worked out.

This involved using hire cars. The criminals would hire a car, in some cases by producing false documents such as a forged driving licence, and then it was up to the hire car company to sort out the damage claim with the other driver whilst the criminal could claim for the usual whiplash injury.

A whiplash is an injury that is hard to disprove as usually there are no broken bones or other visible signs of injury and these people researched and knew all about them, and any doctor's examination usually supported the false claims.

I recall that during this investigation I went to the Budget Car Hire firm in High Wycombe and as a result of information I supplied, it was ascertained that five of their vehicles had been involved in these crashes within a year, and incredibly, no-one in the company had twigged that there was a pattern emerging.

On the pretext that I working for the insurance companies I examined some of the criminals cars involved in the accident and generally the damage was fairly light and in my view would not have resulted in whiplash injuries.

The criminals probably got a whiff of information that their claims were subject of investigation because when I had enough information to justify arrests, two were detained in High Wycombe, but the other two and the main instigators had fled the country.

The court case and publicity put a stop to this little scam, at least in High Wycombe.

It is a shame that this type of crime is making a recurrence.

LOOKING BACK

When I joined the Buckinghamshire Constabulary in 1955, I had my police career planned out. I planned to serve five years as a beat constable, five years on the Traffic Department, five years with the CID and my last fifteen years as a village constable, preferably somewhere in the Chilterns or the Vale of Aylesbury.

I completed five years on the beat, eight years on the Traffic Department, and then my plans went wrong. Firstly, by the amalgamation of the Buckinghamshire Constabulary into the Thames Valley Police. This meant I could be posted to places such as Slough, Reading, Bracknell or even Oxford. Secondly, my elevation to the rank of sergeant eleven months later threw my plans entirely out of kilter.

I must admit that my time with the Stolen Car Squad opened up a number of opportunities and provided me with a varied and satisfying sixteen years. However, I still regarded myself as a rustic copper at heart.

In my unremarkable thirty years of service, as far as I am aware, I set three firsts and one last. I was the first officer in the Buckinghamshire Constabulary to a use radar speed meter to secure a conviction for speeding.

I was the first officer in the Buckinghamshire Constabulary to use the breathalyser and to secure a conviction for drunk driving, and I believe I was the first to be promoted from constable to detective sergeant within eleven months. My last was that I was the last person in the newly constituted Thames Valley Police in 1968 to continue to wear his old Buckinghamshire Constabulary uniform.

WHAT HAPPENED AFTER I RETIRED?

After thirty years in the police, and eight years working as a full time insurance investigator, I retired for the second time. Or so I thought!

About three months after retirement, I got a telephone call from an ex-police officer who had set himself up as a freelance insurance investigator. I will call him Wally.

Wally was dealing with an insurance claim submitted by a man who had bought a car in America, exported it from there to France and then shipped the car via a ferry to England, insured it, then a month later it was found burnt out.

Understandably, the insurance company were suspicious. Wally who was dealing with this claim was at a loss as to how to obtain all the necessary information to prove or disprove the claim.

The car was an Acura, a make Wally had not even heard of (The Acura is an American made Honda). He asked me to help. I told him to give me the details and I would get back to him as soon as possible.

Unknown to Wally, standing beside me when he made the telephone call was my good friend, Dwight, a detective sergeant with the California Highway Patrol, who with his wife, was visiting us.

I asked Dwight, who was flying home the next day, if he could do some checks in the USA and he readily agreed.

Dwight came up with the goods. A couple of days later he called me. He had obtained the manufacturer's records, obtained the registration details from the DMV (Department of Motor Vehicles), of the first owner and the second owner who did the exporting. He had found the shipping line on which the car was transported and he had the name of the ship and a copy of the manifest.

Dwight had checked with the NATB (National Automobile Theft Bureau) that the car was not subject of a defaulted hire purchase deal or of an insurance claim in the States, and with the FBI that the car had not been reported stolen in the States.

Dwight faxed all of this information to me.

In the meanwhile I had also made enquiries. I had a good friend who was the manager of ARGOS, the French equivalent of the ABI (Association of British Insurers), and through his contacts, on my behalf, he had ascertained that whilst the car was on the continent it had not been subject of an insurance claim or had been reported stolen in either France, Spain or Portugal, where ARGOS also had offices.

In effect, with my contacts help I had proved that

the car had a clean bill of health, that is, until it was imported into the U.K.

Wally was amazed at the amount of information I had gleaned in such a short period of time, in particular he was intrigued that I had access to the FBI records. I did not let on as to how this information was obtained.

This story highlights the importance of good contacts and inter-departmental cooperation in the investigation of auto crime.

Wally then asked me to work for him as a freelance insurance investigator, usually on the more complex cases and for the next five years I did so until I finally retired in 2001.

FINALLY

I retired from the police on the 19th September 1986, having served for thirty years.

The aforementioned short stories are just a few that I can think of and I am sure with time many more such events could be recalled, so look out for my next book, 'More Ramblings of a Rustic Copper'.

I can say with some conviction that my service, from a somewhat shy and uneducated probationer constable, to the heights of lecturing to over five hundred distinguished persons at Houston on international auto crime, my time in the police had been somewhat surprising and very fulfilling.

ABOUT THE AUTHOR

Now an octogenarian, Brian likes to keep up with the times, researching books, already having produced four volumes of his family history.

His love of writing and stories in general has led him to publish his memoirs, in order that everyone may enjoy, or at least relive, some of the exploits of a young policeman in rural Buckinghamshire and surrounding areas.

Living in South Oxfordshire, Brian still enjoys a healthy and active lifestyle, playing badminton, cycling and trying to keep up with his four grandchildren.

35719405R00155

Printed in Great Britain
by Amazon